Original title:
Dappled Curds Under the Elf Flint

Author: Mirell Mesipuu
ISBN HARDBACK: 978-1-80562-830-9
ISBN PAPERBACK: 978-1-80564-351-7

Marvels of the Night's Embrace

In shadows deep where magic plays,
The moonlit path, a silver gaze.
With stars above in twinkling choir,
Whispers of dreams build gentle fire.

A tapestry of velvet skies,
Where secrets dance, and hope complies.
Each breeze that stirs the quiet air,
Carries a tale, rich and rare.

Amidst the dark where wonders bloom,
Night's beauty casts away the gloom.
In every corner of the night,
Lies an adventure, pure delight.

The owls hoot softly, their lore spun,
In shadows cast by setting sun.
With every rustle, magic calls,
To those who heed the night's enthralls.

So take a step, in wonder lost,
For night's embrace, no warmth is crossed.
Embrace the dreams, let worries fade,
In night's soft arms, be unafraid.

The Glowing Orchard of Dusk

In twilight's glow, the orchard hums,
With fruits of gold that softly come.
Beneath the trees, the shadows play,
As dusk unfolds in rich array.

A breeze wraps round, a gentle sigh,
Painting the sky with hues awry.
Where whispered secrets softly creep,
And dreams awaken from their sleep.

The blossoms glow, like lanterns bright,
In swirling mists of fading light.
Each branch a tale, each leaf a song,
In this serene, enchanted throng.

With every step, a journey made,
In nature's heart, where worries fade.
The orchard calls with charms untold,
A kingdom rich, a sight to hold.

So linger here, let time suspend,
In magic's realm where dreams transcend.
In twilight's arms, be lost awhile,
In the orchard's glow, find your smile.

The Hidden Scroll of Whispered Wishes

Beneath the arch of ancient stone,
A treasure waits, for hearts alone.
With whispers soft, it draws you near,
To secrets held through many a year.

A scroll so old, with ink of night,
Tales of hopes, and dreams in flight.
In every curl, a wish concealed,
In every line, the heart revealed.

With trembling hands, the parchment pressed,
Unlock the truths that once were blessed.
Each word a spark, igniting fire,
A symphony of pure desire.

The voices linger, softly weave,
Encouragement that you believe.
In every wish, a chance to grow,
In hidden scrolls, your dreams will flow.

So quest for light in shadows cast,
With each wish made, you break the past.
Embrace the magic, set it free,
In whispered wishes, be truly thee.

Enchantment Bottled in Radiant Dew

In dawn's embrace, a shimmer bright,
Dewdrops nestle, pure delight.
Whispers held in silken folds,
Stories ancient, yet untold.

A bottle glimmers, secrets deep,
Each droplet cradles dreams we keep.
A touch of magic in the morn,
Awakens wonders, newly born.

From petals fair, the essence drawn,
In every gleam, a brand-new lawn.
The sunlight dances, realms to weave,
In radiant hues, we dare believe.

Each dewdrop spark, a chance to roam,
Through hidden woods, we find our home.
A path of glimmers, soft and sweet,
With every step, our hearts'll beat.

So gather close, this magic rare,
In radiant dew, beyond compare.
Let dreams take flight, unburdened, free,
In every drop, eternity.

The Flickering Tides in Twilight's Glow

As clouds drift low, the sun descends,
Soft whispers play, the twilight bends.
The tides they rise, a rhythmic dream,
In evening's glow, a quiet scheme.

The sea shimmers with whispered light,
In shadows deep, where stars take flight.
With each wave's crest, a secret sings,
Of lost treasures and timeless things.

The flicker of lanterns leads the way,
To hidden shores where secrets stay.
Beneath the moon's celestial glow,
The tides shall dance, the night shall flow.

In every drop, a world unfolds,
Of ancient lore and legends bold.
So let the ocean's song draw near,
In twilight's breath, we shed our fear.

With arms wide open, we greet the night,
In every glimmer, pure delight.
Together, bound by dreams untold,
In flickering tides, we shall be bold.

Tales in the Realm of Gossamer Dreams

In realms where gossamer threads entwine,
The stories spin, a silken line.
With fairy lights that softly gleam,
We wander through a waking dream.

Each whisper floats, a fleeting part,
In every tale, we find the heart.
The laughter echoes, sweet and rare,
A dance of shadows filled with air.

On moonbeam paths, we drift and sway,
Where fantasies paint the skies of gray.
From every dream, a tale is born,
In gossamer threads, we are adorned.

So gather round, in light's embrace,
Let every story find its place.
In hushed reveries, we shall trust,
In dreams' soft whispers, brave and just.

Through tangled webs, our hopes will soar,
With every breath, we seek for more.
In realms of dreams, we join the dance,
With every heartbeat, a second chance.

Enchanted Petals of Moonlit Sighs

Beneath the moon's soft, silken light,
Enchanted petals bloom at night.
Each sigh a whisper, sweet and low,
In fragrant gardens, secrets grow.

The stars in velvet skies do gleam,
A tapestry of whispered dream.
In moonlit shade, the blossoms sway,
With every breath, they softly play.

In twilight hues, their beauty glows,
Awakening stories that the heart knows.
The scent of night, a lover's call,
In every petal, magic falls.

So let the moon guide us near,
In enchanted worlds, we conquer fear.
With every sigh, let spirits rise,
Through petals spun of moonlit skies.

In whispered tones, beneath the stars,
We find our place, where magic chars.
With every heartbeat, love ignites,
In enchanted petals, through the nights.

Mossy Jewels in the Fairy Hollow

In a hollow where fairies play,
Mossy jewels greet the day.
Glimmers of green, a soft embrace,
Nature's treasures find their place.

Twirling leaves in the gentle breeze,
Whispering tales among the trees.
Each step on earth, a quiet song,
In the woods where hearts belong.

Sunlight dances on emerald beds,
While quiet secrets the wild spreads.
Glistening dreams in twilight's sphere,
Awakening hope, dispelling fear.

Beneath a sky of crystal blue,
The fairies' laughter rings so true.
With every shimmer, the world ignites,
In the hollow where magic lights.

Together we wander, hand in hand,
Through the mossy jewels, the fairy land.
A realm of whispers, soft and bright,
In the heart of day or cloak of night.

Beneath the Glistening Silver Fern

Beneath the silver fern so grand,
Where moonlight weaves through emerald strands.
A hidden world unfolds with grace,
In shadows soft, the fairies chase.

Every droplet sings a tune,
Underneath the watchful moon.
Softly glowing, whispers blend,
In the night, all sorrows mend.

Dancing lightly, they twirl and spin,
In shimmering realms where dreams begin.
With laughter bright, they break the gloom,
Bringing life to silence's tomb.

They gather stardust, pure and bright,
To sprinkle joy throughout the night.
In the whispers of the cool night air,
Secrets shared, and hearts laid bare.

When dawn awakes to chase the stars,
The silver fern holds memories ours.
A tapestry of magic spun,
Beneath the ferns, the world is one.

Mirthful Murmurs by the Misty Brook

By the brook where waters gleam,
Mirthful murmurs softly stream.
With every ripple, a tale is spun,
Of hidden laughter, joy begun.

Sunlight dances on crystal flows,
While gentle breezes weave and pose.
Fairy folk in playful races,
Chasing light in secret places.

Frogs croak out a rhythmic beat,
While dragonflies twirl on nimble feet.
By the rocks where stories blend,
Nature's canvas, hugs extend.

Each petal whispers a secret fair,
In the embrace of fragrant air.
Listen closely, you may hear,
The brook's soft laughter drawing near.

As twilight paints the world in hue,
Mirthful murmurs call to you.
In every drop, a wish bestowed,
By the brook where dreams flowed.

Secrets of the Sylvan Veil

In the depths of the sylvan veil,
Ancient secrets linger, pale.
A world untouched by time's cruel hands,
Where magic thrives and nature stands.

The whispers weave through leafy boughs,
While hidden creatures make their vows.
Softly spoken, their prayers rise,
In the embrace of emerald skies.

Moonbeams blush on the forest's heart,
Where every shadow plays its part.
With twinkling eyes and playful glee,
They guard the lore of mystery.

Beneath the canopy, dreams take flight,
With echoes of the stars so bright.
In every nook, a story waits,
By the whispered calls of woodland fates.

Together we seek the veiled delight,
In the forest where spirits light.
Secrets shared in hushed refrain,
Through the sylvan veil, we'll remain.

Whispers of Cream Beneath Mossy Rocks

Beneath the rocks where shadows play,
Soft whispers dance through morning's grey.
The cream of clouds in twilight streams,
Embraces earth with gentle dreams.

A secret world in silence lies,
Where magic lives and nature sighs.
Each breath a tale of leaves and streams,
In quietude, the heart redeems.

In hidden nooks, the fairies peek,
Their laughter light, their language sleek.
Among the roots, soft voices call,
In lively whispers, they enthrall.

Oh, linger here, let time stand still,
And let the woodland grant its will.
For in this realm, our spirits blend,
With nature's heart, a timeless friend.

Shadows Dancing on Enchanted Pastures

In fields where shadows twirl and sway,
The whispers of the past at play.
Each gentle breeze a lover's touch,
In twilight's grace, we feel so much.

The flowers bloom with vibrant tales,
In colors bright, like vibrant sails.
The nightingale sings soft and sweet,
Where love and magic gently meet.

As moonlight spills on emerald ground,
The essence of the night is found.
Each step we take, a playful glide,
In this enchanted world, we bide.

The stars above, a guiding flame,
Each silver spark, a whispered name.
In dreams we dance, in dreams we soar,
In enchanted pastures, forevermore.

Moonlit Glimmers in Woodland Glades

In woodland glades where shadows sigh,
Moonlit glimmers paint the sky.
They twinkle bright on leaves of gold,
In secrets whispered, dreams unfold.

A silver path through trees entwined,
Where ancient roots and magic bind.
Up high a chorus, pure and clear,
Nature's song for all to hear.

As critters stir in twilight's glow,
The gentle streams begin to flow.
In each soft ripple, life anew,
Moonlit glimmers cast in dew.

Oh wander here with heart in hand,
In shadowed glades, take time to stand.
For under stars, we find our way,
In moonlit dreams, forever stay.

Rustic Delights of the Hidden Glen

In hidden glens, beneath the trees,
Rustic delights drift on the breeze.
With every step, a treasure found,
In wildflowers that cloak the ground.

The crackling fire at dusk's embrace,
Where laughter mingles with the space.
The scent of earth, of pine, and sage,
We weave our tales, we turn the page.

Crickets hum a soothing tune,
As stars awaken, one by one.
Each note a gift from night's sweet song,
In twilight's arms, we all belong.

So gather 'round, let stories flow,
Of all the places we will go.
In hidden glens, let hearts ignite,
Rustic delights in friendship's light.

Elfin Shadows and Golden Moons

In the twilight glow of golden moons,
Elfin shadows dance to ancient tunes.
Whispers soft in the cool night air,
Magic woven, everywhere.

Glimmers twinkling on dew-kissed leaves,
Secrets hidden among the heaves.
Mysteries spun in silken threads,
Along the paths where the soft light spreads.

Voices echo from the forest deep,
Where the weary wanderers seek their sleep.
Underneath stars that gently gleam,
Weaves the fabric of a timeless dream.

With silver beams through boughs that sway,
The night unfolds in a splendid display.
Elfin laughter breaks the serene,
A symphony of the unseen.

And as dawn spills its rosy hue,
The shadows fade, yet magic's true.
In every corner of this land,
An echo left by a gentle hand.

A Gathering Beneath the Whispering Pines

Beneath the pines where secrets sigh,
Creatures gather as the night drifts by.
A tapestry of stars unfolds,
Stories woven, each one told.

The moonlight spills like silken threads,
Over the ground where the night flower spreads.
Gentle breezes carry their tales,
In the hush of woods where magic prevails.

Eyes aglow with a tender light,
Bonds of friendship in the soft twilight.
Hearts entwined in whispered cheer,
Together they conquer every fear.

As laughter dances on the breeze,
They find solace among the trees.
In the sanctuary of nature's embrace,
Love flourishes in this sacred space.

And when the dawn begins to rise,
With pink hues stretching across the skies,
They gather close for one last song,
A vow that their spirits shall carry along.

The Splendor of Celestial Ripples

In the quietude of a starlit sea,
Celestial ripples call to me.
Waves of silver, soft and light,
Whisper secrets through the night.

Shimmering paths of the cosmic flow,
Illuminate the dreams we sow.
Each ripple sings of distant lands,
Threads of fate in unseen hands.

The universe hums a gentle tune,
As stardust settles beneath the moon.
A dance of colors, bright and bold,
Echoes the stories long retold.

Embers sparkle in the sky's embrace,
An invitation to explore this space.
For in the vastness of the night,
Lies the essence of pure delight.

So let us wander where dreams reside,
On the crest of waves, we'll glide.
In the splendor of celestial care,
Our spirits soar, forever rare.

Shining Essence of the Forest Decree

In the heart of woods, a whisper's plea,
The shining essence of a forest decree.
Ancient trees with their wisdom stand,
Guardians fierce of this enchanted land.

With emerald leaves that dance in the breeze,
They hold the stories of ages with ease.
Tales of magic in each bark's twist,
The history written in twilight mist.

Soft moss carpets the forest floor,
Where light streams in through the leafy door.
Every critter, from great to small,
Plays a role in the grandest ball.

The brook chimes in with a sparkling song,
As creatures skitter and flit along.
Every rustle, a page turned anew,
In the tale of the woods where wonders brew.

And when the night drapes its velvet gown,
The forest wears its starry crown.
In this realm where dreams take flight,
Echoes a promise of endless light.

Elfin Echoes of a Creamy Dream

In a meadow soft with dew,
Whispers of the night took flight.
Elfin laughter in the breeze,
Wrapped in silken, starlit light.

Creamy clouds drift overhead,
Carrying secrets, sweet and light.
Where every shadow softly sighs,
And dreams take wing, like birds in flight.

Moonlit glades where wishes bloom,
Underneath the ancient trees.
Elfin echoes call and hum,
In a world where hearts find ease.

Bubbles dance in crystal streams,
Carved by magic's gentle hand.
And in the warmth of dreamy beams,
We trace our paths through softest sand.

A creamy dream that lingers still,
In whispered tales of night and day.
For every heart that dares to will,
Will find its way, and light the way.

Beneath the Canopy of Ancient Trees

Beneath the boughs where shadows play,
Time drips like honey, sweet and slow.
A symphony of rustling leaves,
Where whispers of the forest flow.

Mossy carpets hug the ground,
Embracing secrets of the earth.
In this haven, peace is found,
As magic spins from ancient mirth.

Sunlight kisses emerald hues,
Painting portraits on the bark.
In the silence, wisdom brews,
A journey born from hidden spark.

In twilight's glow, the shadows grow,
As stars emerge with twinkling grace.
Beneath the canopy, we know,
Our souls entwined in nature's embrace.

The ancient trees hold tales untold,
In their roots, the magic stirs.
And with each breath, we dare to hold,
The essence of their timeless purrs.

The Unseen Feast at Twilight's Edge

When twilight spreads her velvet cloak,
And stars gleam in the silver night.
A banquet set for those who seek,
The hidden joys just out of sight.

Moonbeams twirl on fanciful plates,
Filled with treats from dreams once shared.
Laughter mingles with the breeze,
As magic weaves through the prepared.

Spectral guests of all delights,
Gather 'round in mystery.
With every bite, the heart ignites,
In feasts of pure enchantment free.

Dancing flames in candle-glow,
Embers whisper tales of yore.
At twilight's edge, where wishes flow,
A hidden world lies at the door.

So come and taste the starlit fruit,
Among the shadows, glowing bright.
Where unseen feasts lay waiting still,
Awake to dreams in gentle night.

Enchanted Dairy and Mystical Light

In the dairy of the dreamers,
Where the cream flows like a stream.
Each drop a tale of wondrous warmth,
Crafted from the sweetest dream.

Maggie churns with gentle hands,
Her laughter fills the air around.
With milk from stars and honeyed plans,
Each potion sings with joy profound.

Underneath the lanterns' glow,
Mystical light begins to dance.
As creatures great and small do show,
United in the ghostly trance.

Curds and whey in harmony,
A banquet fit for faerie kin.
And whispers weave through tapestry,
Of all the dreams that dwell within.

So gather near, let tales inspire,
In enchanted dairy's gleaming sight.
For in the warmth of this desire,
We find our way in mystic light.

Glittering Leaves of Luminous Lore

In the woods where whispers sway,
Leaves of gold dance in the play.
Secrets held in every hue,
Stories waiting to break through.

Beneath the boughs, the shadows creep,
In ancient tales that softly sleep.
The moonlight strokes each emerald pane,
Revealing magic wrapped in grain.

Time stands still in the dimmest glade,
Where memories of giants are made.
Each fluttering leaf a voice so bright,
Calling forth the deep of night.

Crisp air hums with charms untold,
As folklore weaves through threads of gold.
Nature sings with every breeze,
In harmony with ancient trees.

So wander here, where dreams ignite,
And let the forest hold you tight.
For in the glow of leaves so rare,
Lies a world beyond compare.

Serenades in the Heart of Evening

As twilight wraps the day in cowl,
The stars peek out, the crickets howl.
Soft notes drift on the evening air,
In melodies of sweet despair.

Shadows linger on cobbled streets,
Where lovers stroll in whispered beats.
The moon bestows a silvery glow,
As secrets of the heart bestow.

A breeze brings tales from distant lands,
Of dreams and hopes in gentle strands.
Each sigh a longing, softly shared,
In harmony, two souls prepared.

Memories dance in candlelight,
While time weaves strands of pure delight.
The night, a canvas deep and wide,
Where hearts converse and fears collide.

So let the music fill your soul,
With every note, let passion roll.
For in the serenade's sweet thrall,
The evening whispers to us all.

Flickering Bodies of Ethereal Whirl

Upon the edge where starlight flares,
Flickering forms spin in the airs.
Ghostly dancers, shadows entwined,
In a rhythm strange yet perfectly aligned.

Glimmers flit like whispers of dreams,
Threaded through the silvery beams.
Twilight's breath, a gentle tease,
Twirling through the weightless breeze.

They sweep and sway with whispered grace,
In a transient and timeless space.
Where echoes linger on the brink,
In every glance, the worlds do blink.

Silent laughter fills the night,
As fireflies join the fleeting flight.
Each heartbeat shares a secret frame,
In the flicker of the eternal flame.

So chase the night, embrace the wild,
Become again the dreamer's child.
In ethereal whirls where magic spins,
The dance of existence truly begins.

Tales from an Undulating Meadow

Beneath the sky's expansive dome,
An undulating field finds home.
With daisies bright and grasses tall,
A tapestry of life's sweet call.

Whispers skate on evening's breath,
As stories of the wild find rest.
Each ripple holds a world unseen,
In the meadows' vibrant sheen.

Caterpillars shed their skin,
And dance beneath the soft-violet din.
The sun dips low, a golden friend,
As day and dusk begin to blend.

The brook gurgles with tales to tell,
Of fleeting moments where spirits dwell.
Nature shares her quiet pride,
In each heartbeat where dreams abide.

So wander through this tranquil glade,
Where every dream has softly laid.
For in these tales of softest sway,
Lies the beauty of another day.

Celestial Array in the Secret Glen

In the glen where shadows play,
Stars above softly sway,
Moonlight bathes the gentle brook,
Secrets held in every nook.

Crickets sing their evening tune,
Beneath the watchful eye of moon,
Whispers dance on evening's breeze,
Holding magic with such ease.

The trees wear crowns of silver light,
Guardians of the tranquil night,
Dewdrops glimmer on the grass,
As if to wish the hours pass.

Beneath the sky, both deep and wide,
Where dreams and wishes collide,
Mysterious hues ignite the air,
A celestial show beyond compare.

In this glen, where peace is spun,
All souls gather, one by one,
The magic lives within this place,
Forever holds a warm embrace.

Twinkling Spirits on the Hoarfrost Path

On the path where frost does gleam,
Twinkling spirits weave a dream,
Shimmering light in twilight's wake,
Guiding footsteps gently take.

Beneath the trees, so tall and wise,
Whispers of old magic rise,
A dance of mist in frosty air,
Cloaked in blankets soft and rare.

Each step leads to hidden glades,
Where time slows and never fades,
Glistening webs spun tight with care,
Holding stories whispered rare.

The night is bright, a silvery hue,
With stars above, a wondrous view,
Life unfurls, a twinkling cheer,
In the heart of winter clear.

On this path, where spirits play,
The magic lingers night and day,
And as the dawn begins to break,
A world reborn, for love's own sake.

Softest Delights in the Faerie Glade

In the glade where faeries dance,
Softest delights weave a glance,
Petals whispered on the breeze,
A world afloat with fragrant trees.

Glistening wings in sunlight's glow,
Twirl and dip, a radiant show,
Laughter echoes, pure and bright,
Circling round in joyous flight.

Buttercups hold dewdrops' charm,
Caressing kin with gentle warmth,
In secret nooks where dreams are spun,
Endless stories just begun.

Frolic 'neath the emerald boughs,
With every promise nature vows,
A tapestry of bliss and grace,
As faeries smile in their embrace.

Here in this enchanted land,
With tender hearts and outstretched hands,
Life's sweetest gifts are always near,
In the faerie glade we hold dear.

Herbal Whispers and Timeless Tales

In the garden where herbs entwine,
Whispers echo, soft and fine,
Each leaf carries a story vast,
Of ancient legends, shadows cast.

Thyme and sage in dawn's embrace,
Breathe life into this sacred space,
With every scent, a memory swell,
Of whispered truths and tales to tell.

Rosemary's touch, a gentle hand,
Guiding wanderers through the land,
A potion brewed with love and care,
Mending hearts that lay bare.

The air is rich with softest hues,
Brewing magic in every muse,
With every root and bloom that stirs,
Magic lives in whispered slurs.

So gather round, both young and old,
For every herb a tale unfolds,
In this garden where dreams conspire,
Timeless tales that never tire.

Moonbeams and Magic in Fairyland

In shadows soft, where whispers dwell,
The moonbeams weave their silver spell.
Through glades of green, in secret night,
The fairies twirl in pure delight.

Beneath the stars, their laughter spins,
A dance of joy where magic begins.
With twinkling eyes, they gather round,
In every heart, their dreams are found.

Soft petals bloom, kissed by soft light,
In harmony, they take to flight.
With every twirl, a breeze takes hold,
Their stories bright, forever told.

Through tangled woods, with gentle grace,
They hide their charms in time and space.
The night is rich with secrets deep,
While all the world is fast asleep.

In fairyland, where wonders gleam,
Reality fades like a fleeting dream.
In moonlit hours, their magic sings,
Across the glades, on silver wings.

Enchantment by the Shimmering Pond

By the pond where lilies sway,
Soft echo whispers night and day.
Reflecting stars in waters clear,
The fae gather, full of cheer.

In twilight's glow, enchantments bloom,
A fragrant breeze, dispelling gloom.
With every ripple, secrets glide,
As dreams gather 'neath the tide.

Gentle fairies, by moonlight's grace,
Splash and play in a hidden place.
With silver nets, they catch the light,
And dance until the dawn's first sight.

From every leaf, a melody,
In harmony, they sing with glee.
The trees stand tall, a watchful band,
Guarding magic by the pond's strand.

When morning comes, they softly fade,
Yet linger still, in memories laid.
By the shimmering pond they rest,
In hearts of those who feel them best.

Sylphs Dancing on Mellow Mirth

In fields of gold, where soft winds sigh,
The sylphs arise, to dance and fly.
With laughter sweet, they weave the air,
As sunlight glistens on their hair.

On gentle breezes, they swirl and twirl,
With whispers soft, like ribbons whirl.
They paint the sky in colors bright,
A canvas filled with pure delight.

Among the flowers, their secrets bloom,
With playful hearts, they cast off gloom.
In every petal, a story spins,
Where joy begins and never ends.

With each soft laugh, the world is new,
As magic dances, pure and true.
They gather 'round the ancient oak,
In every smile, a promise spoke.

As daylight wanes, they bid farewell,
But in our dreams, their spirits dwell.
Shall we remember their dance of mirth,
And carry forth their vibrant worth?

The Hidden Feast of the Woodland Realm

In secret glades where time stands still,
The woodland creatures gather at will.
With toadstools round, the feast is laid,
In twilight's arms, magic is made.

With acorns sweet and berries bright,
They share the joy of the coming night.
Each critter brings a fragrant dish,
A banquet born of nature's wish.

The owls hoot softly, their wisdom clear,
While fireflies dance, spreading cheer.
With tales of old, they pass the time,
As stars above begin to climb.

Beneath the canopy, shadows play,
Each heart enwrapped in nature's sway.
The nightingale sings her gentle tune,
Echoing dreams beneath the moon.

When feasting ends, they raise a cheer,
For friendships forged, forever dear.
In woodland realms, where magic thrives,
The hidden feast in hearts survives.

Whispers of Moonlit Reflection

In the stillness of night's embrace,
The moonlight dances, soft and bright,
Casting shadows that take their place,
In the heart of a world bathed in white.

Whispers echo, secrets untold,
Upon the breeze like a gentle sigh,
A tapestry of stories unfold,
Under the watchful, silvery eye.

The trees stand silent, wise and tall,
Guardians of dreams that flicker and fade,
As night wraps all in its velvet shawl,
And memories linger, sweetly laid.

Footsteps echo on the path ahead,
Each step unfolding the tales of yore,
In this realm where the lost have led,
A magic woven on destiny's floor.

With each breath, the night holds tight,
The breath of stars in the vast expanse,
Whispers of hope in the silver light,
A moonlit reflection, a timeless dance.

Shadows Beneath the Woodland Canopy

Beneath the arch of ancient trees,
Where sunlight dapples the mossy ground,
Shadows twist upon the breeze,
In the quiet place where magic's found.

Whispers echo, soft and low,
As leaves rustle in harmony's song,
A tranquil dance in a gentle flow,
In the woodland realm where dreams belong.

The ferns sway gracefully, a ballet,
While creatures stir in the fading light,
Life reveals its wondrous display,
In the embrace of the coming night.

Violet hues begin to bloom,
Softening edges of day's decree,
As shadows fold into deepening gloom,
Creating a world where spirits wander free.

A story woven in twilight's weave,
Of hope and dreams that can never die,
Beneath the trees where you can believe,
In the magic held beneath the sky.

Enchanted Cream in the Twilight Glade

In twilight's glade where the stream does flow,
The air is sweet with whispers of cream,
Golden light begins to glow,
As evening weaves a soft daydream.

Petals flutter in a gentle sigh,
While fireflies begin their dance,
A symphony of sparks on high,
In a world where magic finds its chance.

The brook hums tunes of olden time,
Glimmers of stories through water's grace,
Whispers of peace, a soothing rhyme,
In the heart of this enchanted place.

Beams of starlight peek through the trees,
Guiding wanderers on their way,
As night unfolds its velvet keys,
Unlocking dreams where shadows play.

Embrace the calm of this twilight scene,
For in every breath, a promise lies,
A taste of life's enchanted cream,
In the glade where wonder never dies.

Fluttering Dreams on a Sunlit Stream

A sunlit stream meanders bright,
Where dragonflies dance in midair grace,
Each flicker holds a glimpse of light,
Reflecting dreams in a tender space.

The waters ripple in playful tones,
Laughter carried on the breeze,
A symphony of nature's moans,
As hearts awaken, full of ease.

Golden rays weave through the trees,
Painting shadows on the ground,
Fluttering dreams ride the gentle breeze,
In a world where joy is found.

With each soft splash, a story blooms,
Bathed in warmth of the sun's embrace,
Chasing away the twilight glooms,
In the heart of this magical place.

So let your spirit take to flight,
On the journey that nature inspires,
For every flutter holds delight,
In the song of the sunlit choirs.

Luminous Lullabies in the Glade

In soft glow of twilight's embrace,
Flickering lights dance with grace.
Whispers thread through leaves so light,
Echoes fading into the night.

Moonbeams kiss the sleeping ferns,
While magic in the stillness churns.
Each shadow holds a tale untold,
In the glade where dreams unfold.

Stars weave secrets in the air,
Crickets sing a sleepy prayer.
Petals close in soft retreat,
Nature's heartbeat, slow and sweet.

Breezes carry sighs of peace,
As night's lullabies never cease.
Rest now, 'neath the twilight's song,
In this haven we belong.

With every breath, the magic starts,
Luminous lullabies in hearts.
The glade whispers, soft and low,
Where timeless dreams of wonder flow.

Fae Serenade in the Starlit Grove

In the grove where shadows blend,
Fae twinkling lights begin to send.
A serenade drifts through the trees,
Carried gently on the breeze.

With laughter born from ancient lore,
They dance through openings evermore.
Among the roots, their mischief glows,
Creating magic in twinkling shows.

Softly spoken, words dance high,
Whispered secrets beneath the sky.
Misty veils float through the night,
As starlight bathes the grove in light.

Each note a thread in time's own loom,
Weaving joy in the midnight bloom.
Nature sways to their soft tune,
Fae serenade beneath the moon.

As hearts align in dreamlike trance,
The starlit grove begins to dance.
With every twirl, the world transforms,
In this place where true love warms.

The Glittering Cauldron of Nature's Brew

In depths of woods where secrets lie,
Beneath a canopy, shadows sigh.
A cauldron bubbles, verdant and bright,
Nature's brew in mystic light.

Roots entwined like fingers old,
Whispers of stories, cherished and bold.
Leaves like parchment, inked with dreams,
Flowing softly in moonlit streams.

Each droplet sparkles, a treasure rare,
Brewing wonders that linger in air.
Fable and fantasy swirl and twine,
In nature's heart, a magic divine.

Herbs of healing, petals of charm,
Nature's gifts, they never harm.
With each potion, spirits rise,
As daylight fades, the magic flies.

In the cauldron, all things blend,
A tapestry that knows no end.
From earth's rich soil to sky so blue,
The glittering cauldron brews something new.

Beneath the Canopy of Whispered Wishes

Beneath the branches woven tight,
Where dreams drift softly into night.
Whispers linger, secrets shared,
In this haven, all are spared.

Moonlight spills like silver thread,
On wishes whispered, softly bred.
Children of starlight, hopes ignite,
Glowing gently in darkened light.

Every heartbeat, nature calls,
Echoing through the ancient halls.
A symphony of nightbirds sing,
The magic of the forest spring.

With every wish, the shadows dance,
Bathed in wonders, wrapped in chance.
Beneath this canopy so wide,
In dreams, the universe could abide.

So close your eyes, believe the tale,
Whispers carried on the gale.
Wishes kindled, desires blend,
In this refuge, hopes ascend.

Shimmers of Time by Nature's Call

In whispers soft, the twilight falls,
Where every leaf a secret calls.
The river hums a gentle tune,
As shadows weave, and moments swoon.

In glades where ancient stories sleep,
The ground is rich, the promises deep.
Each ray of light a fleeting sigh,
As day gives birth to night's soft cry.

The trees stand tall with knowing grace,
Their roots entwined, a warm embrace.
In every breeze, a heartbeat flows,
A breath of life where magic grows.

So take a step through nature's gate,
In every pause, a chance to wait.
For time is more than ticking hands,
It's captured in these vibrant lands.

Embrace the dance of dusk and dawn,
For in these moments, dreams are drawn.
A shiver runs through leaf and branch,
In nature's grasp, we find our chance.

Ambrosial Glistens of the Evening Light

Beneath the arch of fading skies,
The stars awake with sleepy eyes.
Each glimmer holds a tale untold,
As dusk unfolds its cloak of gold.

The flowers sway in fragrant dreams,
As moonlight spills in silver streams.
In every petal, glow and gleam,
A symphony of night's soft theme.

Each shadow whispers secrets near,
While echoes sing for those who hear.
The world transformed by evening's gleam,
A tapestry of starlit dream.

As twilight paints the skies anew,
The air is kissed with fragrant dew.
In this embrace of night's delight,
We find our peace, our hearts take flight.

So linger here, in nature's grace,
In every glint, a warm embrace.
For every heart, a place to shine,
In evening's glow, our spirits climb.

The Ethereal Dance Among Starlit Woods

In woods where shadows hold their breath,
The night unfolds, a dance with death.
Each rustling leaf a secret keeps,
As nature's pulse in silence leaps.

The silver beams through branches play,
In midnight's hush, the fairies sway.
They stir the air with laughter light,
A waltz beneath the cloak of night.

The whispers of the ancient trees,
Are woven into nightly breeze.
Each branch adorned with twinkling gems,
A tapestry of nature's hems.

In every rustle, tales arise,
The stories borne from starry skies.
With every step, a dream ignites,
In harmony with endless nights.

So come, my friend, and lose your way,
In woods where darkness meets the day.
Where stars and shadows intertwine,
And hearts find strength in love divine.

Whimsy in a Hallowed Glen

In glens where sunlight dances free,
The flowers bloom with jubilee.
Each color bright, a canvas wide,
Where dreams and wishes bloom inside.

With laughter woven in the air,
The fae spin tales without a care.
They flit like butterflies in flight,
In happiness, both day and night.

The brook sings sweet, a bubbly tune,
Reflecting glimmers of the moon.
In every ripple, glimpses show,
Of magic thriving, ebb and flow.

Where nature's heart beats ever bold,
In whispers soft, the stories told.
In every step, a world unfolds,
A hallowed journey, pure as gold.

So pause and breathe this vibrant scene,
In every moment, joy unseen.
In whimsy's grasp, our spirits soar,
In hallowed glens, our hearts explore.

Light and Shade in the Faerie Dell

In the dell where shadows dance,
Fleeting whispers weave their chance.
Moonlight spills on emerald grass,
As time itself begins to pass.

A flicker here, a shimmer there,
Secrets held in twilight's air.
Golden glows through trees will thread,
Enchanting tales of those who tread.

With each step, a silent song,
Calling to those who wander long.
Petals flutter, soft and light,
Beneath the vast and starry night.

Luminous creatures softly play,
Guiding dreams that float away.
In this realm of light and shade,
Heart's desires will not evade.

So linger here in nature's fold,
Within the stories yet untold.
For in the magic of the dell,
We find our place, our wishes swell.

Creamy Chimeras in the Moon's Embrace

In the night where dreams take flight,
Chimeras swirl in silver light.
Candy hues in moonlit streams,
Filling hearts with sweetened dreams.

Whispers ride the midnight air,
Creamy visions everywhere.
Sailing boats on chocolate lakes,
Where magic brews and laughter wakes.

Cotton clouds in pastel skies,
Balloons with colors that mesmerize.
Creatures frolic, soft and real,
Each a truth that makes us feel.

Underneath the starry glow,
Imagination starts to flow.
In this world both strange and new,
Pure delight comes into view.

So set your sails on dreams tonight,
Chasing shadows in the light.
Let creamy chimeras take your hand,
And guide you through this wondrous land.

The Sylph's Soft Refrain Beneath the Boughs

Beneath the boughs where whispers blend,
The sylphs will sing and softly send.
Melodies like gentle streams,
Carrying the heart's pure dreams.

In shaded glades where sunlight leaks,
They twirl and twist, with secrets speaks.
Guiding hearts through leafy maze,
Swaying gently in a daze.

With filmy wings in emerald light,
They sparkle through the coming night.
Every note a story spun,
In harmony, they come undone.

Grounded where the earth is warm,
They weave enchantments, sweet and calm.
So listen close, let them unveil,
The sylph's song, a wondrous tale.

In every breeze, their whispers cling,
A soft refrain that makes us sing.
Beyond the boughs, the magic swells,
Drawing dreams from secret wells.

Dreams Drifting on a Fragrant Breeze

In the garden, fragrant and wide,
Dreams drift forth, a gentle tide.
Petals kiss the morning light,
Floating free, a wondrous sight.

Where lavender and roses bloom,
Whispers fill the fragrant room.
Breath of hope, a soft caress,
Carrying song in sweet excess.

Breezes curl through mossy nooks,
Stirring tales from ancient books.
Each sweet breath, a tale unfolds,
Of love and mysteries untold.

So chase the dreams upon the air,
Let sweetness linger everywhere.
For in this moment, time stands still,
Drifting dreams, an endless thrill.

With every sigh and every breeze,
We find the magic that won't cease.
In fragrant waves, our spirits soar,
As dreams drift gently evermore.

Celestial Tides of the Forest Floor

In twilight's glow, the shadows dance,
Whispers of magic in each chance.
Moonlight weaves through branches high,
A symphony beneath the sky.

The river sings, a secret tune,
Reflecting dreams beneath the moon.
Stars twinkle like enchanted sprites,
Guiding hearts on starry nights.

Mossy carpets, soft and deep,
Cradle secrets that we keep.
Each petal falls, a heart at rest,
Nature's cradle, ever blessed.

In every rustle, magic stirs,
The ancient woods, where time blurs.
Echoes linger, soft and bright,
In the embrace of silver light.

As evening falls, the world stands still,
Nature whispers, hearts to fill.
A tapestry of gentle sighs,
Where dreams awaken, soft and shy.

Fables of the Glade's Hidden Delicacies

In the glade where the wildflowers bloom,
Creatures scurry through shadow and gloom.
Delicacies of earth and sky,
The humble treasures that pass us by.

Berries glisten like rubies bright,
Clutched by thorns, a daring flight.
Secrets of sweetness, hidden in leaves,
Nature's canvas, fantasy weaves.

Mushrooms peek with curious grace,
A fairy ring in a secret place.
Tales unfold in the softest hues,
Whispered lore in the evening dew.

The breeze carries scents of the earth,
A fragrant dance of life and birth.
Every morsel, a tale untold,
Of sunlit days and nights so bold.

Savor the flavors of the glade's heart,
Where time stands still, where wonders start.
In the embrace of nature's song,
We find the place where we belong.

Secrets Shared in the Quiet of the Grove

Beneath the oak, in shadows cast,
Whispers linger, memories past.
The grove hums with stories old,
In every sigh, a truth unfolds.

Leaves confide in the gentle breeze,
While time drips slow, a sacred tease.
Cloaked in twilight, secrets dwell,
In each silence, magic fell.

Moonbeams paint the forest floor,
Revealing paths to dreams galore.
A cautious fox, a darting hare,
Hide their fables, hearts laid bare.

With every rustle, whispers raise,
Stories spin in twilight's haze.
The grove holds truths in every leaf,
Nature's ink of joy and grief.

In the hush, a pact unfolds,
Time and earth, their secrets told.
Hand in hand, we roam the night,
Beneath the stars, a shared delight.

The Gentle Caress of Nature's Bounty

Morning breaks with a golden light,
Flowers stretch, embracing the sight.
Breezes dance through fields so wide,
Nature's blessing, our joyful guide.

Honey drips from the comb's delight,
The sweet embrace of day and night.
Every seed a promise sown,
In fertile hearts, our dreams have grown.

Waves of grain, a shimmering sea,
Whispers of what is yet to be.
The rustling leaves hum a tune,
Cocooned in warmth, we shall attune.

Gathering below the ancient trees,
Fruits await with the gentlest tease.
Nature's feast upon the land,
In the palm of life, a gentle hand.

As twilight cools, the stars arise,
We find our magic in the skies.
Nature's bounty, a sweet embrace,
In every heartbeat, love finds its place.

Gentle Twinklings of the Wildwood Sprites

In the hush of night, they come alive,
A dance of lights in the twinkling leaves,
Tiny guardians with hearts so bright,
They weave their magic, the forest believes.

Mirthful laughter in the cool, soft air,
A shimmer here, a glow over there,
Ripples of joy in each delicate flight,
Whispering secrets beneath the moonlight.

They gather round the ancient trees,
Befriending shadows, invoking the breeze,
Sparkling eyes as they share their tales,
Of forgotten worlds where wonder prevails.

With petals and stardust they patch the night,
Filling the dark with their soft, gentle light,
Each flicker a promise of dreams that ignite,
The very essence of magic in flight.

Oh, to wander beneath their guise,
Among the whispers of starlit skies,
For in the heart of the wildwood fair,
The sprites share a glimpse of their world with care.

The Enchantment of Quiet Glimmers

In a meadow kissed by twilight's grace,
The quiet glimmers begin to glow,
Delicate hues in a secret place,
That few have wandered, and fewer know.

With whispers of hope in the dusky air,
Their soft luminescence gently sways,
Tiny sparks in the evening's care,
Mastering shadows in a dreamlike haze.

A tapestry woven with silken thread,
Each flicker spins stories long as the night,
Of moonbeams dancing, of wishes said,
In the warmth of their softly glowing light.

The earth hums sweetly, a lullaby sings,
As starlings and crickets join in the throng,
A chorus of wonders that evening brings,
In symphonies crafted where spirits belong.

Oh, linger here in their soft embrace,
As the world fades gently into the dream,
For in these moments of tender grace,
The quiet glimmers weave life's radiant seam.

Cauldron of Light Amongst the Boughs

Deep in the grove where the wild things dwell,
A cauldron simmers with magic bright,
Blending the whispers of the ancient spell,
In a frothy brew of shimmering light.

Leaves overhead twist in a gentle dance,
Cloaking secrets beneath their shade,
While faeries laugh, caught in a trance,
As the cauldron bubbles, enchantments made.

A sprinkle of stardust, a touch of dew,
With petals plucked from the blooms that sigh,
Each ingredient cherished, every drop true,
Gifts from the forest beneath the wide sky.

Around the fire, the creatures convene,
Sharing tales that the night has spun,
In the heart of the wild, a magical scene,
Where shadows and light whimsically run.

So heed the call where the light is found,
For in this cauldron, dreams intertwine,
In each bubbling whisper, hope is profound,
A potion of joy, forever divine.

Swaying Fables of the Luminous Wild

In a world where the fireflies play,
Swaying gently to the night's sweet tune,
Fables spin through the branches' sway,
As stars peek out behind the moon.

With every breath, the tales unfold,
Of loves that linger and friendships bright,
Each flicker a chapter, each shimmer told,
In the embrace of the velvet night.

The brook gurgles softly, a melody clear,
While wisdom from the willow takes flight,
Nature's whispers for all who draw near,
Guiding us deeper into the light.

From roots of the past to the leaves of dreams,
Every story entwines with delight,
In the luminous wild where the heart redeems,
And the glow of the dusk paints the night.

So gather around and share your own tale,
Let the spirit of wonder endlessly flow,
For in this wildwood where magic prevails,
The swaying fables of life brightly glow.

Blossoms of Light in Eternal Enchantment

In gardens where the fairies dwell,
Petals whisper stories to the dell.
Glowing orbs of silken hue,
Dance beneath the sky so blue.

Breezes carry sweet perfume,
Awakening dreams from slumber's gloom.
Each bloom a wish, so pure, so bright,
A promise held in soft twilight.

Moonlit paths of silver thread,
Guide the wanderers, once misled.
With every step, enchantment grows,
As magic in the stillness flows.

In twilight's gaze, the secrets lie,
Of whispered hopes and lullabies.
Stars weave tales in the night,
Illuminating hearts with light.

Eternal blooms of vibrant grace,
Shimmer softly in their place.
In this realm of endless dream,
Life unfolds like a gentle stream.

The Veil of Light in Emerald Dreams

In emerald fields where shadows dance,
A veil of light gives dreams a chance.
Whispering secrets of stars above,
Awakening echoes of timeless love.

Through glades where ancient whispers dwell,
Nature spins her wondrous spell.
Softly murmuring through the trees,
Laughter flows upon the breeze.

With each dawn, a canvas bright,
Painting hopes in morning light.
Each petal glimmers, soaked in dew,
A world anew, enchanted, true.

The forest sings of days gone by,
While sunlight weaves through branches high.
In emerald dreams, the heart does soar,
Finding magic on every floor.

As twilight falls, the veil takes flight,
Wrapping all in gentle night.
Love's embrace within the seams,
We dwell in these emerald dreams.

A Tapestry of Starlight Canopy

Woven threads of starlit skies,
A tapestry where wonder lies.
Each star a story yet untold,
In midnight's fabric, woven bold.

Softly shining, the night unfolds,
Casting magic as it beholds.
With every glance, the heart will stir,
Whispers of worlds that shadow blur.

The moonlight dances on the stream,
Reflecting dreams which softly gleam.
In that glow, our spirits soar,
A cosmic dance forevermore.

Celestial wonders greet the dawn,
As nature sings its timeless song.
Wrapped in light, we drift and sway,
In this vast, enchanted play.

A tapestry of dreams unveiled,
Where every soul is gently hailed.
Underneath this starlit sea,
We find our hearts, forever free.

Underneath the Ocean of Shadows

In depths where silence softly flows,
An ocean waits, where shadows pose.
Beneath the waves, a world concealed,
A tapestry of dreams revealed.

Whispers of secrets drift in the tide,
Where mysteries of the deep abide.
Flickers of light, a subtle spark,
Illuminate the enveloping dark.

Coral castles and seaweed trails,
Tell tales of lost and ghostly sails.
In tranquil currents, hope does bloom,
Cradled softly in the muted gloom.

Each ripple carries stories grand,
Of forgotten lives on shifting sand.
The ocean sighs a lullaby,
Cradling dreams as time slips by.

Within the shadows, magic waits,
Unlocking all the hidden gates.
For underneath, the heart can find,
A treasure trove of the gentle kind.

Eldritch Feasts Beneath Fairy Brow

Beneath the moon, where shadows dance,
We gather close, in secret trance.
With whispered lore of ancient kind,
The eldritch feasts, unseen, unwind.

Chanting songs of yore and fate,
The twilight sky opens the gate.
Amongst the ferns, where spirits play,
We feast on dreams that fade away.

A shimmering path of silver light,
Leads us gently through the night.
From hidden glades, the shadows creep,
Secrets beckon, while others sleep.

With goblets raised to skies above,
We drink deep the nectar of love.
In laughter shared, our hearts take flight,
Bound by spell in the still, soft night.

And when the dawn begins to break,
We hush our songs for morning's sake.
Yet in our hearts, the magic stays,
Eldritch feasts shall bless our days.

Softly Glow the Beings of Wood

In gentle glades where sunlight weaves,
The woodlands hum with whispered leaves.
Amongst the moss and ancient trees,
The beings glow with tranquil ease.

A flicker here, a shimmer there,
They dance and sway in fragrant air.
With glistening skin and eyes so bright,
Softly glowing in morning light.

They cradle dreams within their hands,
And weave the threads of ancient lands.
Their laughter mingles with the breeze,
A symphony that soothes and frees.

With every step, their essence sings,
As nature bends and softly clings.
In dappled shade, they slip and glide,
Where secrets meet the forest wide.

With hearts as light as drifting seeds,
They nurture all the world's deep needs.
In twilight's grasp, their warmth bestows,
A tender glow that never goes.

Elusive Murmurs on Wisping Winds

Where wisping winds bring tales anew,
Elusive murmurs drift on through.
They wrap around the starlit night,
And entwine dreams in softest flight.

A spoken breeze of whispered lore,
Invites the stars to dance once more.
Each secret carried on the air,
Holds echoes of an unknown prayer.

Through twilight's hand and dusky vale,
They weave a song, a haunting tale.
With voices shrouded, shadows play,
Amongst the moonbeams, lost and stray.

The sighing leaves will bend and sway,
To catch the breeze that knows no sway.
With every gust, their stories blend,
The murmurs skip, around the bend.

In night's embrace, hearts listen close,
To all the whispers, faint yet gross.
For in the silence that descends,
Lie secrets shared, the night intends.

Glowing Grace in Nature's Embrace

In nature's arms, where wildflowers grow,
A sacred dance begins to flow.
With petals bright, and scents divine,
We find our peace, our hearts entwined.

The sunlight spills like golden wine,
Casting a glow that's pure and fine.
Each shimmering leaf, each gentle sparrow,
Sings of the grace that's surely narrow.

The rivers laugh as they cascade,
In nature's throne, we're gently swayed.
With every breeze, her soft embrace,
We lose ourselves in time and space.

In twilight's blush and morning hue,
The world unfolds, so fresh and new.
With every dawn, we're born again,
In glowing grace, we live, refrain.

And when the night wraps round us tight,
We hold the stars, a dazzling sight.
Together, lost in nature's art,
We glow as one, in love's sweet heart.

Elfin Echoes in the Meadow Mist

In the embrace of morning fine,
Elves weave spells through dew and shine.
Whispers dance on gentle breeze,
Nature hums in verdant trees.

Over hills where shadows creep,
Secrets from the ancients seep.
Sparkling laughter fills the air,
Magic weaves its silver snare.

With each petal's blush anew,
Moments caught in emerald hue.
Forgotten tales of love and strife,
Echo softly, breathe in life.

Gossamer wings aloft they soar,
Toward the sun-swept forest's door.
Elfin echoes blend with light,
Chasing dreams through day and night.

In every glen where wild things play,
Stories linger, come what may.
As dusk unfolds her velvet skein,
Elfin heartbeats call again.

Melodies of the Hidden Dell

In a dell where shadows blend,
Songs of old begin to mend.
Charming notes on whispering winds,
Echo through where silence spins.

Moonlight drapes the veiled trees,
Filled with secrets, hushed with ease.
Crickets chirp a lullaby,
Nestled 'neath the starlit sky.

Mossy stones and silver streams,
Weave a tapestry of dreams.
Every rustle, soft and light,
Holds the promise of the night.

With each chirp a tale unfolds,
Of valiant hearts, of love, of gold.
Hidden dell, so full of grace,
Keeps the fables in its embrace.

Soft the breeze as night prevails,
Murmurs weave through ancient trails.
Melodies of soft refrain,
In this dell, we'll dance again.

Glimmering Spirits in the Twilight Realm

As shadows merge with twinkling light,
Spirits gather, taking flight.
Glimmers dance in quiet glades,
Whispers weave through twilight shades.

Each moment swirls with mystic grace,
In this enchanted, hidden place.
Stars adorn the velvet sky,
Luxury in every sigh.

Tender hues of dusk arise,
Silken threads in starlit skies.
Winds of fortune gently blow,
Secrets shared by those who know.

With every heartbeat, glimmer bright,
Illuminating paths of night.
Chasing shadows, bold and brave,
Lost in dreams, together save.

Glimmering spirits drift and play,
Guiding souls who've lost their way.
In twilight realm, we find our peace,
And in the stillness, fears do cease.

Luminescent Fables of the Forest Floor

Beneath the boughs where secrets dwell,
Luminescent stories swell.
Fables whispered on the breeze,
Echo softly through the trees.

Beneath the stars, the world aglow,
Every shadow starts to flow.
Crimson leaves and golden light,
Craft a world both strange and bright.

In every thicket, dreams take flight,
Woven in the fabric of night.
Mushrooms glint like stars on ground,
Tales of wonder all around.

Nature writes its epic prose,
In every petal, every rose.
With each heartbeat, stories spin,
Grotesque, lovely, dark and thin.

Through canopies of ancient trees,
Fables float upon the breeze.
Luminescent, we embrace,
The magic found in nature's grace.

The Enchantment of Softened Whispers

In twilight's breath, where shadows play,
Soft whispers dance, as night meets day.
An owl calls out, a gentle sigh,
While stars above begin to fly.

The moonlit path, a silver thread,
Where secrets weave, where dreams are fed.
With every step, the world unfolds,
A tapestry of tales retold.

In hidden glades, the wild things roam,
They call the forest's heart their home.
A rustling leaf, a spark of light,
Awakens magic in the night.

Whispers carry on the breeze,
An ancient song among the trees.
With every rustle, spellbound air,
A promise made, a vow laid bare.

So linger here, in twilight's gleam,
Where every moment stirs a dream.
The enchantment lies in whispered tales,
Where magic thrives and hope prevails.

Hushed Secrets in a Sylvan Realm

In the heart of woods, a silence falls,
Where every shadow softly calls.
The ferns unfurl, with secrets hold,
In whispered tones, their stories told.

Beneath the boughs, the stillness sighs,
As twilight paints the evening skies.
Each rustling leaf, a breath of fate,
Unfolding dreams, both small and great.

A brook flows gently, its voice a hush,
Amidst the ferns, in twilight's blush.
It speaks of time, both lost and found,
As nature weaves her tales profound.

Soft shadows creep, as night descends,
The forest knows where magic blends.
With every heartbeat, wisdom breathed,
In hushed embrace, we're gently wreathed.

So wander deep in this sylvan song,
Where every whisper has belonged.
In secret realms, beneath the trees,
Lie stories bound to set us free.

Tales from the Lichen-Covered Stone

Upon a stone draped in nature's cloak,
Lay tales long forgotten, yet softly spoke.
Lichen whispers in shades of green,
Earth's gentle scribes, where life has been.

Each crevice holds a memory's thread,
Where time meanders, a silent spread.
The moss beneath, a verdant bed,
Cradles the stories that sunlight shed.

From humble roots, the giants rise,
With branches reaching for distant skies.
Every shadow, a tale of yore,
Held in silence, forevermore.

So heed the whispers from stone's embrace,
In every crack, the echoes trace.
For nature speaks in riddles deep,
Her secrets promise, her magic keep.

In lichen's glow, let your heart roam,
Discover wonders, make them home.
For every stone, a story holds,
A whispered truth that never folds.

Where Faeries Weave with Dewy Threads

In twilight hours, the faeries play,
With threads of dew that kiss the day.
They twirl and leap on petals small,
In a shimmering dance that binds us all.

Their laughter rings like bells in flight,
As they paint the world with pure delight.
A glimmer here, a sparkle there,
In every breeze, their magic's flair.

Amidst the blooms, they spin their dreams,
With whispered wishes and moonlit beams.
Their gentle hands craft night's embrace,
In softest hues, they weave with grace.

So tread lightly on this sacred ground,
Where faeries hide, and dreams are found.
In starlit glades, let spirits sway,
And join the dance till break of day.

For in this realm, where wonders blend,
The faerie magic knows no end.
With every thread, a story spun,
In dewy dreams, we all are one.

Wandering Whispers in the Twilight Wood

In shadowed glades where secrets dwell,
Whispers drift like distant bell.
The trees, they sigh with ancient lore,
As moonlight spills upon the floor.

A breeze unfolds a tale untold,
Of wanderers brave and spirits bold.
With every step, enchantments weave,
In twilight's grasp, we dare believe.

The brook hums low a tender song,
Where echoes dance, and shadows throng.
Through tangled roots and ferns so green,
A world awakens, yet unseen.

Each fluttering leaf, a silent plea,
For those who seek, a way to be.
In twilight's arms, the heart will stir,
With whispers soft, we start to blur.

As night descends, the magic grows,
In every sigh, the forest knows.
With wand'ring hearts, we find our place,
In twilight's wood, a warm embrace.

The Iridescent Bloom of Gentle Night

In gardens where the shadows bloom,
The glimmers chase away the gloom.
Petals glisten like starlit streams,
In the embrace of velvet dreams.

Each flower whispers secrets bright,
Of magic spun in silver light.
Their fragrance lingers, soft and sweet,
A promise made where lovers meet.

The moon above, her watchful gaze,
Illuminates the night's soft haze.
Beneath her glow, the world feels right,
In harmony, we greet the night.

Gentle breezes weave through the air,
Holding tales of love and care.
In every corner, beauty thrives,
The gentle night, where dreams arise.

With every breath, we feel the pull,
Of magic rich and ever-full.
In twilight's garden, hearts belong,
As stars compose their midnight song.

Reveries in Celestial Tranquility

Beneath the vast, embracing sky,
Where whispers of the cosmos lie,
We find our hearts in dreams enshrined,
In solitude, our souls aligned.

The stars, like lanterns, flicker bright,
Guiding us through the veil of night.
In silence deep, the world unfolds,
As ancient tales of starlight told.

Each comet's tail, a fleeting glance,
Of wishes spun in cosmic dance.
In quietude, we seek the grace,
Of fleeting time, a warm embrace.

The universe, a tapestry,
Of woven dreams and mystery.
In every heartbeat, life's refrain,
In celestial calm, we find our gain.

As stars align, our hopes take flight,
In tranquil realms of endless night.
With every thought, the heavens guide,
In reveries where love abides.

Harmonies of the Hidden Grove

In quiet groves, where shadows play,
The whispers of the trees convey,
A song of life, in harmony,
That dances on like melody.

Each rustle carries nature's tune,
A serenade beneath the moon.
In every breeze, a story flows,
Of hidden paths and whispered woes.

The fireflies spark in joyous flight,
Painting dreams in soft, warm light.
With every glimmer, night unfolds,
A magic wrapped in forest gold.

The brook's gentle laugh, a soothing balm,
In still moments, the world feels calm.
Each step is met with nature's cheer,
In hidden grove, all is sincere.

With every heartbeat, life's refrain,
We find our way through joy and pain.
In harmony, we weave and mend,
In hidden groves, we find our friend.

Hidden Treats in the Realm of Shadows

In the moonlit glen where secrets lie,
Whispers of sweetness drift and sigh.
A tinkling laugh from behind the trees,
A cardamom breeze on the evening's breeze.

Goblets of nectar, shimmering bright,
Eager to dance in the velvet night.
Each berry plucked, a story to tell,
A taste of magic in the old oak well.

Ghostly figures that flicker and sway,
Join in the feast as shadows play.
Laughter erupts from creatures of lore,
As hidden treats invite us to explore.

Crimson petals, soft as a sigh,
Gathered so carefully, just like a spy.
A handful of dreams in a dainty cup,
Raise it to the stars, and look up, look up!

So linger awhile, let wonder unfold,
In the realm of shadows, a tale to be told.
Each hidden delight, a mystery spun,
In the tapestry of twinkling fun.

Echoes of Whimsy at the Edge of Night

The clock strikes softly, a gentle chime,
Gather the whispers, weave them in rhyme.
Dancing through dusk on gossamer threads,
The echoes of whimsy where laughter spreads.

A flicker of starlight above the glade,
Shadows that flicker and softly fade.
Frolicsome spirits twirl in delight,
At the edge of the magical, shimmering night.

Here beneath branches that sway and bend,
The secrets of twilight can blend and mend.
With each passing breeze, hear laughter call,
A symphony woven, enchanting us all.

Neighbors of silence, they twinkle and glow,
Treasures of dusk in the twilight's flow.
Gathering stories the moon softly pens,
Each echo a memory that never ends.

So dance in the shadows, embrace every sound,
For echoes of whimsy in night can be found.
With glee in our hearts and stars shining bright,
We sing to the magic that dwells in the night.

Mystical Medley of Nature's Alchemy

In the heart of the forest, where wonders abide,
Nature's sweet alchemy flows side by side.
With petals that shimmer and leaves that gleam,
A mystical medley, the wild wood's dream.

Riverbanks shimmer with silver and gold,
Legends of nature in spirals unfold.
Moss-covered stones pulse with ancient grace,
In every nook thrives a colorful place.

Swarms of bright fireflies dance in the air,
Whispers of secrets hidden with care.
With laughter and song the crickets awake,
A symphony sweet, a magical wake.

Under the arch of the sprawling trees,
The elixir of life flows with the breeze.
Dew-kissed blossoms in the morning light,
An alchemist's dream, pure and forever bright.

So wander, dear friend, through this vibrant scene,
Where nature's own magic weaves joy in between.
In every breath, let the wonders unfurl,
Embrace the alchemy, let your heart twirl.

Potions of Cream and Enchanted Glimmers

In the depths of the kitchen, so cozy and warm,
Bubbling cauldrons with a mystical charm.
Stirring up potions of cream and delight,
With enchanted glimmers that twinkle at night.

Sprinkle of sugar, a dash of pure spice,
A whisper of starlight, oh, once or twice.
Cinnamon swirls in a dance with the air,
Creating a concoction so wondrous and rare.

A pinch of the moonbeam, soft like a sigh,
Handful of dreams from the sweetened sky.
Frothy and sweet, the elixirs rejoice,
In laughter and love, we find our true voice.

Ovens are glowing with warmth from within,
Each potion assembled, where magic begins.
Taste the creation, let flavors entwine,
A world of enchantment in every line.

So gather your friends, let the magic unfold,
With potions of cream, we'll be bold and be told.
In twilight's embrace, we'll sparkle and shine,
Each sip's an adventure, so divine, so fine.

The Glowing Wreath of Enchanted Hues

In twilight's grasp, the colors blend,
A wreath of light, where shadows bend.
Each petal whispers secrets old,
Of ancient magic, bright and bold.

A dance of hues on misty trails,
A melody of nightingale's wails.
The air is thick with dreams so true,
As stars align in vivid view.

With every flicker, stories gleam,
A tapestry of light, a dream.
A shimmering path through woods of grace,
Where hope and wonder interlace.

The night unfolds, the spirits sigh,
Beneath the veil of endless sky.
A glowing wreath, a timeless spell,
In every heart, its journey dwells.

Reverie by the Glimmering Stream

By the glimmering stream, where willows bend,
Silent whispers of the water send.
Reflections dance in silver light,
Carrying secrets through the night.

Softly flow the dreams we keep,
Lulled by the current, deep and sweet.
A world of echoes, laughter clear,
In nature's arms, we hold so dear.

The stars above in velvet grace,
Illuminate this tranquil place.
With every ripple, time stands still,
We listen close, the night does thrill.

Breath of twilight, soft and warm,
Guiding hearts like a gentle charm.
In joyous reverie we unite,
By the stream's glow, beneath the night.

Of Hidden Bowls and Twinkling Stars

In woods around, the lanterns glow,
Hidden bowls where secrets flow.
Twinkling stars, a cosmic choir,
Igniting dreams with every fire.

Gather 'round, the stories told,
In whispered tones, both brave and bold.
A soft enchantment fills the air,
As laughter mingles with the fair.

Mysteries twinkling in the sky,
As wishes soar and never die.
Each twinkling bowl, a treasure found,
Of hopes and dreams forever bound.

The night, a canvas, dark and bright,
With strokes of magic, pure delight.
In shadows deep and starlit beams,
We chase the echoes of our dreams.

Fragrant Breezes in a Spectral Grove

In a spectral grove where spirits play,
Fragrant breezes drift and sway.
Petals soft, like silken threads,
Weaving tales where magic spreads.

The air is filled with whispered cheer,
A fragrant dance, the night draws near.
Each blossom sings with heart so light,
A harmony to greet the night.

In twilight's breath, the shadows flirt,
With every rustle, hearts are hurt.
But joy remains, a glimmer bright,
In fragrant winds, they take their flight.

The spectral grove, a sacred space,
Where every soul finds its place.
Together woven, hand in hand,
In fragrant breezes, we shall stand.

www.ingramcontent.com/pod-product-compliance
Ingram Content Group UK Ltd.
Pitfield, Milton Keynes, MK11 3LW, UK
UKHW021315280125
4330UKWH00005B/276

Japanese for Travellers

Japanese for Travellers

A Journey

KATIE KITAMURA

HAMISH HAMILTON
LONDON

HAMISH HAMILTON

Published by the Penguin Group
Penguin Books Ltd, 80 Strand, London WC2R 0RL, England
Penguin Group (USA) Inc., 375 Hudson Street, New York, New York 10014, USA
Penguin Group (Canada), 90 Eglinton Avenue East, Suite 700, Toronto, Ontario, Canada M4P 2Y3
(a division of Pearson Penguin Canada Inc.)
Penguin Ireland, 25 St Stephen's Green, Dublin 2, Ireland (a division of Penguin Books Ltd)
Penguin Group (Australia), 250 Camberwell Road, Camberwell, Victoria 3124, Australia
(a division of Pearson Australia Group Pty Ltd)
Penguin Books India Pvt Ltd, 11 Community Centre, Panchsheel Park, New Delhi – 110 017, India
Penguin Group (NZ), cnr Airborne and Rosedale Roads, Albany, Auckland 1310, New Zealand
(a division of Pearson New Zealand Ltd)
Penguin Books (South Africa) (Pty) Ltd, 24 Sturdee Avenue, Rosebank, Johannesburg 2196, South Africa

Penguin Books Ltd, Registered Offices: 80 Strand, London WC2R 0RL, England

www.penguin.com

First published 2006
1

Copyright © Katie Kitamura, 2006
Illustrations by Asako Masunouchi

The moral right of the author has been asserted

Set in 12/16.5 pt Monotype Dante
Typeset by Rowland Phototypesetting Ltd, Bury St Edmunds, Suffolk
Printed in Great Britain by Clays Ltd, St Ives plc

A CIP catalogue record for this book is available from the British Library

ISBN 0–241–14289–x

For my family

Acknowledgements

I am very grateful to David Godwin and Simon Prosser for their patience and insight. I would also like to thank Francesca Main, Juliette Mitchell and Sarah Savitt; Sophie Fiennes, Harland Miller, Sean O'Hagan, Ekow Eshun and Katherine Zoepf.

Contents

25 March 2001, 9.46 p.m.   1

The Big Sun   9
  Place: Tokyo, Japan

20 March 1995, 7.52 a.m.   73

The Bubble   81
  Place: Osaka, Japan

15 August 1945, 11.59 a.m.   171

The Atomic Aftermath   177
  Place: Hiroshima, Japan

25 March 2001, 9.46 p.m.

When he is standing as he is now, head tilted back before melting into a slow roll of the neck, pink tongue poking out from between his lips before retreating again, he is likely to send an instinct of unease starting through the mind of his opponent. Doubt will occur, a thought slow and painful, and then they will have lost already, before the bell is rung or the fight begun. When he is standing as he is now, feet planted squarely in his corner, body slack and casual, it is impossible to believe that Kazushi Sakuraba can be defeated, and it is for this certainty that they gather by the thousands to watch him.

Across him in the ring stands a young Brazilian fighter called Wanderlei Silva. As a fighting proposition, he is a perfectly conditioned map of spheres, half spheres and relentless straight vectors. Each muscle dovetails tightly one into the next, and with Silva, things once released – whether it is his devastating roundhouse kicks, his hard stomps or his slamming knees to the head – must roll towards their designated conclusion, no matter the cost or peril. If Sakuraba works laterally, spider frisking across his web, then Silva hurtles forward with the inevitability of the lance. And it is this determination that Sakuraba must harness and expose as Silva's weakness – for Silva has no other weakness.

They have packed out the Tokyo Dome, fans of the fighting sport, to witness which will be stronger: laxity or tautness, laterality or verticality, Japan or Brazil, but there is not much doubt in their minds that their hero cannot be beaten. It is, after all, his game, and he has written the very terms of the game's brutality through his apparent uninterest. And so these hundred thousand fans are not so very nervous; they do not believe that fate can let them or Sakuraba down. All across the stadium they are settling further into their seats, elbows propped on knees in a stance of comfortable anticipation. There is nothing they enjoy more than the privilege of watching their hero perform.

In their separate corners the two fighters are turning round, slow and cautious, senses adjusting to the heightened sensitivity that forms a constituent part of the fighting ring – the immaculate detailing of cold air on skin, the touch of glove and the hard hollow clapping of hands, feet bouncing slow on the mat. Their ears are keen to the subtle sounds all around, the solitary cheering of an impatient fan in the left side of the second tier, the meticulous layering and intersecting of the announcers' voices, moving through the air in different languages and rhythms, pronouncing their names, their fight records, their strengths and their provenance. Then the bell rings, and the fight begins.

A roar leaps out with the ringing of the bell, but then the stadium falls silent as, within seconds, Kazushi Sakuraba, the man who can't be beaten, the man who has never known the darkness of a knockout or the choke of a tight submission, falls to all fours. He remains there, head down and bleeding from the face as the Brazilian fighter punches and kicks, dances and lunges and taunts him. The silence extends for several long moments, a carefully pieced mosaic of a thousand individual silences, through which the hard slaps of flesh hitting flesh can be heard. Then suddenly that fragile silence erupts into the fragments of a screaming more frenzied than before, and the crowd is on its feet.

Down in the ring, body crouched low to the ground and trembling, eyes swelled shut, face blistering, the fallen fighter sighs. A soft sigh, slipping out from his mouth as a whisper and hanging heavy on the air before him. And as he crouches there, body absorbing a hailstorm of blows, he abruptly perceives the blessedness of the knockout, the sanctity of oblivion. Through his groans, now coming heavier, now coming faster, he smiles, just for a moment, because it is so strange – being stopped, and darkness so close. From across the ring, the referee sees that smile, and then he knows, as he watches, that Sakuraba is getting killed. He is not merely losing, he is not merely being beaten, he is being killed, slowly and systematically.

And so, swallowing hard, he steps in to end the

fight. Doctors flock into the ring, and the referee looks on in wonder as they miraculously enact a dirty resurrection. He watches as Sakuraba comes back to life to address the crowd, limbs bleeding, face raw and swollen like the faces of the drowned. He listens as the suicidal request for a rematch is hailed by a blood-thirsty crowd that loves its hero even more in defeat and recklessness, knowing all the while that once Saku-raba exits the stadium stage he will collapse and remain in collapse, so many bridges of consciousness fallen.

Sakuraba disappears down the long gauntlet leading out of the stadium. The referee looks up at the crowd, screaming in fear and enthusiasm. Something has come undone in that bright spangled mass seething heavy beneath the lights; some sky has fallen. The announcer looks bewildered, the promoters stand helpless and hurrying, and there is no telling how long this con-fusion will last. Then, from inside the ring, the Brazilian fighter throws his head back and screams, *'I love Japan!'*

The promoters stare at him dumbfounded, and instinctively security men move forward. Ringside, a row of men in expensive pressed suits avert their gaze. They wait, nervous and uncertain, as the crowd hesitates. Then a trembling begins in the belly of the stadium, spreading slow to the walls and mounting in register. And so the triumphant fighter says it again, and then again, arms held up and head flung back so that his body is nearly bent double – *'I love Japan! I love Japan!'* – and when he straightens again, fist shaking the winner's trophy, muscles numb and head spun by vertigo, there is nothing touching him but the noise of the crowd's roar.

THE BIG SUN
Place: Tokyo, Japan

I arrive in Japan for what is to be a long stay, a reply to the imperative of recent illnesses in the family (my father's long and continuing recovery from cancer, my grandmother's quickening decline into the twilight of old age; my sense that I have, in Japan, a host of lost relatives). And it is somehow appropriate that this journey should start on a train – trains being an old obsession of my father's, touched with the dust of the years running from childhood to adulthood and then to middle age, those selfsame years that took him from Japan to America, and then back again to Japan.

Burrowed drowsily in the centre of a non-smoking

coach – illogically sandwiched between two smoking carriages, so that the acrid pong of cigarette smoke drifts in as the carriage doors slide open and then close again – I sit aboard the express train running from the suburban outskirts to which all airports are exiled, towards the pulsing centre of Tokyo. Weighted down with its cargo of returning *salarymen* and the occasional family or two, bursting with fatigue and luggage, the train pulls out of the station at Narita Airport and into a misted morning light, already burning off into a hazy winter noon.

As it gathers its slow momentum, the train's placid efficiency is many miles and decades away from the laborious straining of the trains that occupied my father's childhood imagination. Those trains – the trains that tracked across the landscape of post-war Japan, and then also the movie trains that burst out of Hollywood, their celluloid coaches somehow always destined to go off track – affected him so that even when he was older, his vision of happiness flanked the course of some imaginary railway, lodging itself inside the inarticulate bliss of watching phantom coaches, sprung from the canister of childhood and sweeping by according to a regular timetable.

And so it must be through some longstanding empathy with my father that I too have always had a particular inclination towards train journeys, so that they conjure up for me the most longstanding romance of all, that of childhoods known and unknown. And now, newly disembarked from the flight between London and Japan, I find myself observing the strange timelessness that will often declare itself towards the end of long journeys, the product of accumulated fatigue and abandonment. Gradually, it swells through the rocking motion of the train's body, therein finding its rhythm, perhaps because these trains were always more a part of me than I realized.

I always have a feeling of displaced recognition upon returning to Japan, a place that is not my home, and yet for which I often find myself feeling something more than homesickness. It was maybe the wreckage of my father's old obsession with trains that led, via the resultant American professorships in civil engineering, to this state of being. The second child of Japanese immigrants, I was born and raised in California, and brought up mostly American – though in hidden, quiet ways that only showed themselves later, also partly Japanese.

Then, some sixteen years after I was born, my parents made a belated return to their native country. My brother remained in California, I went away to an East Coast university and later moved to London for my graduate studies, and as a family we tacitly agreed to inhabit different time zones. It began, though, with my father. He needed, it seems, to return to the trains of his childhood, to their carriages, to the spinning of their wheels and the shifting of their gears. Perhaps he always knew there was going to be some kind of return; perhaps that was why my brother and I grew up in a household that was never entirely certain whether it was going to remain in America or return home, and why, as a family, we were in some sense always bound to live across different continents, and in different patches of land.

A young couple move down the carriage aisle, steps jolting according to the swaying of the train. My ear listens idly as she speaks over her shoulder; he responds in slow grunts, and their conversation – not simply their spoken words, but the language of their gestures, the floating of hands, the flickering of eyes – comes to me in a dulled clarity, apart from fluency and only partially apprehended. Several minutes later, when the train conductor passes through, I speak to him in a gummy Japanese, words spilling out unsharpened. But he understands me well enough, and everything about his crisp uniform, from the weave of its navy fabric to the stitching on the white gloves, bears with it an air of old familiarity, so that I feel a steady sense of inexplicable recognition, of *déjà vu* not previously seen.

They are both – the young couple and the train conductor – part of a Japan towards which I bear an intimate curiosity, a curiosity that travels in the company of a contrary hesitation. They are part of a Japan that is muffled, speaking in hushed tones and appearing in the half-light of dream corridors. Drawn through this world there is perhaps a dull feeling of regret – the awareness of relatives, cousins my own age hardly known, dead or ageing grandparents whose affection is based on kinship more than knowledge, the consciousness of childhood memories that were so long displaced, so long illegible, that they finally drifted into the fog of a growing forgetfulness. But there is also the growing expectancy of arriving in a place that is part known, part forgotten and part present with a particular richness of being. And it is for this feeling of anticipation, as much as any other, that I travel to come back home.

As the train launches into its long approach towards Tokyo, that sleepy eagerness shakes its head with particular force, and I remember that my cousin is due to meet me on the platform when I arrive. It was almost precisely like this on my last visit to Tokyo, perhaps more than a year earlier. I had collected my bags, and when I stepped off the train she was waiting there, paused before the precise carriage door from which I emerged, waving a casual hand as she stepped forward to help me. She was, then as now, one of my lost relatives, but she seemed unaware of this fact, and there was no quality of lostness to her bearing as she wrestled a bag from me with a casual flip of the wrist, embraced me and then motioned impatiently for me to move out of the way of the passengers bottlenecked behind me in the door of the carriage. Moments later she was striding down the platform, turning her head a lazy half-turn to check that I was following.

And it occurred to me, as I watched the slow swivel of that half-turn, that my cousin was what might be termed a certain version of Japanese. She belonged to the youth generation, the new age of Japanese boys and girls who suddenly seemed ubiquitous in Japan. Thickly thronging the streets, a kaleidoscope of implacable rightness, they and their cool could be seen everywhere. They exhaled cool, lurking on a street corner and flicking the red glowing end of a cigarette to the ground. Their cool tripped after them as they shopped for vintage clothes, browsing with casual deliberation; it kept them company while they sat alone in a bar, legs hooked tightly over stool, mind drifting to the sounds of anonymous jazz.

They were cool in less favourable circumstances, too. Caught within the constrictions of their cram-school uniforms and weighted down heavily with books; dining out with their middle-aged parents (father: *salaryman*, mother: homemaker), laughing at Dad's jokes, pulling out the chair gentleman-like for Mom; riding their bicycles, gangly-limbed and knees whirling because they were still in their third year of saving up for a moped. They even managed to exude cool working at the local Mister Donut, dressed in the plasticine-yellow uniform and calmly distributing donuts.

The youth population, particularly in the cities, was so uniformly cool that after several days in Tokyo I remember thinking it self-evident that nobody here was performing the (equally arduous) task of being uncool. Something had happened in Japan. Some kind of revolution had taken place, and after the revolution, all the young people had been liberated and sent forth into a sanctioned state of cool. Somewhere, at some point, the ethos that had so united their parents' generation – the principles of hard work and selflessness, obedience and depersonalized ambition – had been traded in for trendy haircuts and ironic T-shirts, limited edition sneakers and vintage handbags.

My mind returns to that first glimpse of my cousin waiting on the train platform, face drawn against the blankness of an anonymous crowd. Her bored expression started in the face and then spattered down around her in the clink of silver wrist bangles, in the loose-curling locks of her hair. Her carefully faux vintage dress gathered in an Empire waist before suddenly flaring out to a stop above her knees. As the train rushed forward, slipping into the platform, she shifted her weight in slouchy leather knee boots, balancing neatly on cone shaped heels. A crescent-shaped leather bag with wryly ironic gold and silver baubles hung heavy from her shoulder.

She was the product of an age that took image as its code, and style as its mantra. The tangible portion of this generation's cool, the part that could be discerned and seized upon, might therefore be said to be in its clothes: in the minute detail of accessories, in the precise folds of sartorial innovation. Japanese boys and girls took style with great seriousness, pitting intuition against vigilance and then deftly plunging through an astonishing range of looks. Bowler hats with surfer shorts, neckties with drainpipe jeans, oversize dinner jackets with cropped trousers and flip flops, loose jeans tucked into worker's boots – they relished the taste of all these things that tipped towards the ridiculous, while managing always to recover their balance and remain perfectly, thoroughly, right. And that style gave them a kind of allure that was quite apart from their beauty. (Oh, but they were also beautiful! The girls with their flawless skin, their coquettish smiles, their narrow hips. The boys with their stylish sobriety, their hair grown longish, their coltish limbs and their dreamy expressions.) It was in pursuit of that allure that my cousin, illuminated by a sense of philanthropic mission, decided to take me shopping at one of the largest department stores in Tokyo.

As the train churns through a wet and pastoral landscape, I lazily recall the details of that shopping expedition – never had the experience of shopping seemed so much an expedition – my mind leaping idly from the slow rocking of this train to that of a Tokyo subway carriage, swaying rough through underground tunnels as it burrows out of the past. Slowly past and present converge; as we rode along, standing and swinging to the jolting of the underground, my cousin explained to me the importance of the department store.

It was, she explained to me, an institution in contemporary Japanese life. It was where young people went to hang out, where harried housewives bought their groceries. It was where elderly folk went when they had a bit of shopping to do and cared to pass the hour trudging down the aisles, murmuring to themselves how everything had changed since the old days, and not for the better either. It was a whirl of activity, people flying this way and that as they made their purchases or maybe just took a long look round. You had to stay on your feet, she warned, just to avoid the bustle of the crowd. And so it was at Takashimaya, the finest and largest of these temples of contemporary consumerism, that we, after a slow and grudging ride on that rough rocking subway, finally arrived.

A young mother careered past, briskly pushing a buggy with a wailing infant seated inside; an old lady shook a fist at her as she brushed by, three generations brought together for an instant before going their separate ways. A pair of schoolgirls in blue and white uniforms walked past, naughtiness written in the wriggle of their hips. Over their shoulders hung enormous shopping bags (Gucci, Prada, Louis Vuitton) and as they passed by, collapsing with giggles, a *salaryman* in search of a birthday present for his wife gave them a look of disgust. Youth today. What was this country coming to?

We had come to a place of things, things to appraise and things to desire. Japan is one of the few places in the world where the public pulse of wanting and the national love of consumption surpass America's. Here, in the department store, the post-war colonization of Japanese culture reached its inevitable apogee. There were people shopping frantically, people shopping listlessly, people shopping accidentally and people shopping with deadly intent. Every imaginable product was for sale here – and many more that were unimaginable. The whole place was animated by the energy of money passing hands, the thrill of purchase, the power of commodity.

Starting from the basement there were the food halls, a subterranean maze of winding corridor and aisle. Piles of food: fresh vegetables, ready-made sushi, fried shrimp and pork and chicken, golden-battered tempura, teriyaki bowls; rice with beans and rice with vegetables, rice with fish and rice just plain; sweets of all description, beggaring description (Japanese pastries, beautified balls harbouring a doughy, sticky centre, cakes done in the French style, covered in fruit and cream and chocolate, individually wrapped cookies nestling in beautiful tins); sweet boiled potatoes and fried potatoes in their slick, sugary glazing; salads – dozens of salads, shrimp and broccoli, Caesar, green, pasta, Chinese chicken, tomato and mozzarella and avocado, all ranged along the length of a single counter; ready-made soup, neatly poured into clear plastic containers and placed into bags with cutlery and folded paper napkins. From their counters, uniformed assistants in pinafores and toques hawked their wares, and as you walked through these narrow aisles, brushing hips with the housewives burdened by their purchases, all that could be heard was the cacophony of their cries, 'Fresh potato, fresh potato. Sweet cakes. New fish. Try my crackers!'

One floor up, there was a hanging gallery of accessories – those anonymous, costly objects drenched in the impersonal scent of One Size Fits All. A hundred variations of the same glove, in leather, in cashmere, in vinyl, in wool, decorated with spangles (for the teenage girls) or plain (for the middle-aged ladies) or maybe just dotted with a single, pert ball of fluff. Wallets, scarves, a whole wall cleverly rigged to display six layers of umbrellas, ranged one atop the other. Handbags; many, many handbags, most of them too refined to endure the brutal whacks dished out on a crowded bus, in a busy street, and none of them big enough to hold much more than a lipsticked handkerchief, a tin of mints, a single, exhausted credit card and a quitter's half-pack of cigarettes.

But we were not here to buy crackers, or potatoes, or even lipsticks and eyebrow pencils – though I was tempted, in the distracted style of material longing. We were here to buy clothes. My cousin hooked me by the elbow and pulled me towards an escalator leading up to the second floor. There we discovered a multitude of garments specific to an age range that accommodated teenagers and young women in their twenties, with some minimal acknowledgement made to those with the gall to stray into their thirties.

They were beautifully produced, and marked low. Two matters of seeming permanence, the Japanese economic recession and the Japanese passion for style, had together resulted in a deluge of massively under-priced, devastatingly trendy clothes. I was assailed by a rush of consumerist agoraphobia as I took in the endless array of shorts, pedal pushers, trousers boot cut, tapered or flared; dresses that were impishly short, elegantly long, sleeveless, strapless, figure skimming and sack-like; shirts and sweaters and scarves. Lost in this dizzying array of preferences, the wary shopper could never be sure of having the right one and was instead condemned to the perpetual uncertainty of peeling clothes on and off, squinting into the mirror, standing on tiptoe and hypothesizing the outfit with heels, on a good hair day, in better light.

And everyone everywhere seemed to be doing precisely this. They were casually trying on clothes, gossiping with girlfriends over their shoulders or through a crack in the dressing room curtain, reapplying lipstick in the mirror or frowning over a disappointing hem. They chatted on their mobile phones as they manoeuvred their head and arms through tight sweaters, a sharp elbow poking through the knit and an industry marvel of a phone moving from hand to hand in balletic tension. Clothes flew off the rack and onto bodies and off them again; moments later, they were folded in glossy shopping bags and jogging out of the store, or else they were back on the rack, awaiting the attention of a new customer. Hands reached for the same item of clothing, retracted in momentary confusion, and then reached out again more ruthlessly, scruples overcome.

I turned to look for my cousin. She was standing some feet away, mobile phone in hand, head and face absorbed in disembodied conversation. Working on an entirely different continuum, her spare hand slowly flipped through a rack of clothes. As I looked up, two teenage girls walked by, the rich physicality of feminine friendship hanging thick in the air around them. Lost in mutual delight, they fluttered across the floor like twin butterflies, then disappeared into a changing room. Near by, three girls of indeterminate age browsed with studied indifference. Speaking a patois of mightily condensed slang, one of them demanded a dress in red rather than white, in patterns rather than plain, in a doubtful two sizes smaller. Wary of offending, the shop girl slowly shook her head; they snorted disdainfully and left. As they moved by, the air flashed with diamanté, lengths of skin-tight denim, sequins and sparkles, the acrid scent of cheap perfume.

Still on the phone, my cousin threw me a pointed look. I ignored her and continued creeping through the aisles, peering at people over racks and through display panels. She crossed towards me and grabbed my arm. I looked at her meekly. She indicated a nearby concession with a grim jerk of the head. Then, using my elbow as a lever, she propelled me to a rack. Obediently, I delved through the dense sheaf of clothes, pulling out shirts and skirts and trying to exude a busy air of cooperative activity.

A shop girl approached and said, inclining her head politely and smiling a friendly smile – *something*, my ear having missed the pattering of her words. I stared at her. She looked back at me, gently puzzled.

I turned and looked helplessly at my cousin. Rousing herself, she momentarily prised the mobile phone away from her ear and flatly declared, 'She doesn't speak any Japanese.' (There was a kind of emphasis on both the 'she' and the 'any', so that it was more like '*She* doesn't speak *any* Japanese. *Not a word.*' Later, my cousin told me I was being paranoid again.)

This announcement seemed to baffle the shop girl even more than my apparent social idiocy. My cousin paused again in her telephone conversation. 'She's, you know – American.'

The girl nodded politely. She continued to smile, but with a more remote enthusiasm. Another girl joined her, and they exchanged secret glances.

I looked at them nervously. One of them smiled very faintly in private amusement.

Despairingly, I grabbed a pair of trousers and a shirt. They fell well wide of a tenable match, and amidst the dozens of garments on the rack, they were incongruously bad. They were even – upon closer examination – possibly *ugly*. They were possibly the only two ugly garments out of the thousands in the store, very possibly the only two ugly garments for sale within the extended archipelago of Japan, even. It was not of such stuff that cool was made. No matter, my cousin had already waved the shop girls over.

'Go on, go and try them on.' She smiled and then turned away, still talking into her phone. The two girls smiled at me with cloying professionalism as I traipsed towards the dressing room, then looked about hopefully for other customers to wait upon. I grunted to myself.

Loosening the curtain, I stepped into the dressing room. Consternation appeared on the faces of the girls, who looked at me, then gestured to my cousin in panic. I froze inside the dressing room, one hand on the curtain, rabbit in the headlights of a speeding social censure.

My cousin bustled over, shop girls in tow.

'You have to take your shoes off *first*.'

Defensively, I spluttered, 'How was I supposed to know that? Nobody told me. How on earth was I supposed to know something like that?'

The girls, heads bent over the soiled carpet inside the dressing room, seemed genuinely horrified. I stared down at my feet, dutifully mimicking their dismay. Muttering to myself, I backed out of the dressing room and bent over to take my shoes off. That done, the shop girls ushered me into the dressing room again, one on each side and with appropriate caution; they had, it seemed, decided upon a more hands-on approach. One of them held up what looked like a jumbo-sized gauze envelope. Moving slowly, she mimed placing it over her head, carefully unfolding the fabric and maintaining rigorous eye contact to check that I understood.

I heard my cousin's voice from the side. 'You put that over your head. You know, to prevent makeup stains.'

'I'm not wearing any makeup.'

She looked at me blankly. 'You're not wearing makeup?'

'No.'

'Why?'

'What?'

'Oh, never mind. Just do it. Otherwise you'll stress them out even more.'

'Fine,' I grunted. I snatched the gauze makeup cover. The shop girl sprang away lightly, only a faint panic showing in her eyes. She closed the changing room curtain with a rattle.

I was left alone with the clothes. For several moments I stood still, looking down at them helplessly. They looked as limp and despairing as I felt, as if they too knew the case was hopeless. Outside, I heard one of the shop girls clear her throat delicately. Gritting my teeth, I started changing out of my clothes.

'You OK in there?' Through the curtain I heard my cousin's muffled voice pause midstream. Then, without waiting for a response, she plunged back into her mobile conversation.

I looked at myself in the mirror. I was dressed in hip-hugging, butt-crunching, red tartan trousers. They flared into an unforgivingly bell-bottomed cut, and conspired to make my legs look as though they belonged to an overweight and improbably nationalistic Scottish pony. The plaid patterning came undone in those choice locations where the fabric was naturally apt to grow a little stretched. For a top, I had selected a bright green cardigan in a fleecy material that looked capable of dyeing everything in the washing machine intensely green, before then fading into colourlessness. Its oversized buttons were moronic, and the tawdriness of the fabric was apparent before a first wash, wearing, or glance.

'Hello?' My cousin tentatively stuck a hand round the edge of the curtain. I looked at the hand. The hand waved dejectedly. 'Hey, can I come in?'

I muttered something that, in the crack between her English and my Japanese, sounded like consent, and she pulled the curtain open. I was indeed a sight to behold, judging from the aghast expressions on the shop girls' faces and my cousin's own undeniable consternation.

'*What are you wearing –?*'

She looked at the shop girls accusingly. '*What* is she wearing?' They shrugged helplessly with uplifted hands, disavowing responsibility.

My cousin sighed and put her hands on her waist. 'Come on,' she said. 'It's not funny. Stop fooling around and take that off.'

'I'm not fool—'

She pulled the curtain shut with a firm and practised motion.

'—ing around,' I said to the curtain.

Squirming my way out of the clothes was itself an endeavour, the static of the green top clinging to my hair and setting it straight on end, the trousers so monstrously tight that it took an inordinate amount of time to peel them down, inch by slow inch; even so, they left long and angry red markings on my legs. Heaving a sigh of relief as I slipped into my jeans and tank top, I heard my cousin busily haranguing the shop girls: '*Who* would wear that kind of purple? . . . This? But the cut on the sleeve is terrible! Here. Let me see that one . . .'

When I emerged from the changing room, she was standing beside a display cabinet covered in clothes, sleeves and slips hanging messily over its edges. A few stray hangers were strewn on the floor.

'We've picked a few things for you to try on,' she said cheerily as she sorted through the selected garments. She raised her head and looked at me. Her brow crinkled.

'What's wrong with your hair?'

'Nothing.'

'OK,' she said reluctantly. She hesitated for a moment. Then, shaking her head, she turned her attention back to the clothes she had amassed, as if for reassurance.

'Here.' She threw an armful of clothes at me. 'Go and try these on.'

'I'm not sure this is a good idea.'

'Look.' She paused. 'Just try these things on. If you don't like them, we can go. Simple as that.'

Sighing, I clutched the clothes to my chest and lumbered back towards the changing room.

'Don't forget to take your shoes off!' she called after me.

My cousin had picked an emerald-green dress with a plunging back and front. A delicate embroidery cut across the fabric, and tiny knots of darkened leather were stitched down round the neck and waist. The dress was stylish, efficient. The fit was perfect. I opened the curtain. My cousin was waiting, arms folded across her chest.

'Much better.'

'What do I do with this?' I held up a gauzy indigo scarf.

'Here.' Stepping forward, she grabbed the scarf from my hand and tied it around my hair, smoothing it down with a deft movement of the fingers. She stepped back, tilting her head to one side in appraisal. 'Yeah. I think that works.' She leaned over to pick up her bag. 'OK, let's go.'

I changed back into my jeans and tank top while my cousin waited outside. I handed the clothes to the shop girls, one of whom trotted off to wrap them. I turned to my cousin.

'How do you do it?'

'Do what?'

'You know – that, with clothes. How do you know what to get?'

She shook her head slowly, then sighed.

The shop girl returned with a glossy shopping bag which she handed to me. I signed the credit card receipt. My cousin thanked the shop girls with brusque politeness before leading me towards the escalators. The time had slipped into the post-work hours, and the store was even more thronged; young women littered the aisles and pressed up together on escalators and in lines, lost in busy conversation, opening their wallets, slipping in and out of clothes. For a brief moment, in the schema of mirror and glass, they were reflected one across the other, and I caught a brief glimpse of my cousin, embedded in that glittering affray. Their multiple images slid across the polished surfaces. Then, in a quick trick of the light, they disappeared altogether.

On the train, sunlight cuts through the overhang of cloud, dazzling the eye. A young man reaches for his sunglasses, pauses, then lowers the blind instead. Just as the blind touches the ledge of the window and his hand moves away, the sun disappears again, and the landscape outside scrabbles back into grey. The young man sighs, then flicks the blind back up. With a snapping motion, the length of blind disappears into the top of the window.

I turn away. The question of where they would go, these boys and girls, when they tired of their shopping and when the day was over, the question of what waited for them on the other side, when they emerged from the darkness of the subway, squinting in the newfound sun, whether it was a part-time job without benefits or the confines of a bedroom long ago outgrown, the question of what truly separated my cousin from me, of what sometimes made her so bluntly unreadable – in the myopic closeness of the moment, that pile-up of questions was blotted out by the glinting surface of their shared aura, by the impression they left trailing in their wake.

That surface was so brilliantly rendered that it very nearly made the question of what lay beneath irrelevant – very nearly, but not quite. The cool that floated over this current generation was a strictly surface thing. It failed to penetrate; it declared itself on the surface, in the fashion of a haircut, in the falsetto vocals of a rock band, in the creation of a façade more complete, more fully imagined, than any conceivable to the generations before. And that exterior, slippery and elusive and surprisingly vital, was at once the screen behind which this generation concealed itself, and also the code by which it was read and revealed.

It was the nature of this paradox that most concerned modern Japanese parents, those mothers and fathers – my aunts and uncles – who stared at their children from across a moat of baffled incomprehension. It was never the precise quality of that surface that was the genuine cause for concern; rather it was the anxiety that this surface was not surface at all, but totality. The internal life of this youth generation was a great unknown, and the real dread was that this opaque surface might itself constitute the sum total of their world.

If that anxiety was especially acute, then that was because these parents believed they were ceding their children a world of firmly established moral principles. From the earliest days of their childhood, in cram schools, private tutorials and music lessons, in the smothering of a heavy pressure to succeed, in the perennial absence of their hard-working fathers, in the count of his overtime hours and the monotony of a vacant chair at the head of the dinner table, these parents taught their children that hard work and achievement was a natural, inevitable state of being. But when the Bubble of the over-inflated Eighties economy burst and national morale plummeted past zero, when fathers across Japan were laid off and household finances spiralled into disarray, when an epidemic of depression and suicide sprang upon the country, these children grew alive to the fact that hard work came with no guarantees, and understood with uncanny prescience that the model they had been taught to follow from their earliest years was crumbling to pieces before their eyes.

They watched silently as their fathers returned, bodies depleted from a lifetime's work. They noted the sudden outbreak of parental quarrelling. They observed the swift death of affluence as the companies that seemed permanent collapsed and the buildings that seemed indestructible fell. They watched as cults of apocalypse and despair seized upon the talent and determination that had suddenly been left homeless. They understood what they were witnessing, as they saw the pride and fortitude of their parents' generation fall away, and blankness sweep into its place.

Outside, the landscape passes from the muteness of greened fields to the irregular murmurings of farmhouses and sheds, from the fragmented articulations of freestanding homes to the slow-gathering pronouncement of suburban streets. And during the course of this gradual acquisition of terrestrial speech, there is now visible in the middle distance the urban pileup of skyscrapers and lights that denotes the noisy proclamation of Tokyo City itself.

A light rain begins, throwing sloppy tears onto the train windows. Condensation slowly clouds the view. A young girl pulls down the end of her sleeve before wiping her hand across the window in a slow and unhurried gesture, leaving behind a fan-shaped clearing on the glass. I sit low in my seat, coat stretched tight across my lap and hands resting folded on its lapels. From across the aisle, over the head of the girl and through that second window within the window,

I watch the drizzling of the landscape, and there is something in the sight of that backdrop that makes me recollect a parallel rain, several years earlier in London.

I was then newly arrived in the city, and growing accustomed to its restless patterns of rain. Reluctant pedestrians were clogging up the exits from the Tube, and on the street, the light had reached an approximate dusk. As I walked from the direction of the library at St Pancras, the rain continued to fall, and I remember that across the street, the bookshops were glowing with warm, dry-looking light. On my side of the street a reluctant renovation was taking place, its sluggish tempo of progress recorded in the irregular collage of fly-posters pasted across boards and wrapped around scaffolding poles, ancient images from a month ago already covered up by this week's release.

Further down the road, another stretch of wall was covered with posters advertising a film. The poster was arresting – a black and white image of schoolchildren solemnly posed in a classroom photograph. Girls sitting in front, boys standing behind them. A severe schoolteacher seated dead centre. The photo was grainy, their faces blurred and haphazard, like images of the deceased. The faces of several children were obscured by lurid red crosses; across the bottom left-hand portion of the poster, an inky emblem read *BATTLE ROYALE*. One of the posters was crumpled and falling forward, and for the sake of the row's consistency, I slapped it back up as I passed by.

I arrived at the cinema to meet a friend; he was waiting impatiently in the lobby.

'You're late,' he said frowning. 'And wet.'

'It's raining.'

'We'll miss the trailers – they're the best part!'

'You always say that, and we never miss the trailers.'

He sighed. 'Anyway, I've got the tickets, let's go in.'

He handed the tickets to the usher, who stared at us dully, glanced with the same expression at the tickets, then muttered something indistinct and directed us downstairs.

'Fine. So.' My friend paused as we reached the bottom floor. 'How was the library?'

'OK.' The poster, expanded in its dimensions but still grainy and indistinct, was hanging prominently on the wall. I stepped up to take a closer look.

'Do you know if the film did well in Japan?'

'I don't know. I suppose so – I mean, Kitano's in it.'

'Hasn't been released in the States, I hear.'

'Why?'

'Apparently it's too controversial.'

'Right.' I paused. 'What does that mean, exactly?'

He shrugged. We filed into the darkened theatre.

'Look,' I said as we sat down. 'Perfect timing. The trailers are about to start.'

He grunted and rolled his eyes at me in the dark. I elbowed him.

'Hey!'

The man next to us coughed.

'You're irritating the other people,' he said reproachfully.

'Shh.'

Trailers flashed across the screen before us. A brief pause of blackness and then the film began, launching into a series of images depicting unruly adolescents engaged in various acts of recreational violence. Then a schoolgirl, covered in blood and surrounded by camera crews. A translated text announced the premise for the film:

> At the dawn of the Millennium, the nation collapsed.
> At 15 per cent unemployment, 10 million were out of
> work, 800,000 students boycotted school. The adults
> lost confidence, and fearing the youth, eventually
> passed the 'Millennium Educational Reform Act' . . .
>
> AKA Battle Royale.

Somebody in the audience giggled, then fell silent.
I shifted in my seat. I smelled wet.

Under the auspices of the 'Millennium Educational
Reform Act', a ninth-grade class was annually chosen
by 'lottery' to participate in the game of Battle Royale.
Now, as we watched, this year's selection of girls and
boys was corralled into a classroom and shown a
menacingly chirpy video explaining the rules of Battle
Royale. They were to be placed on a deserted island,
equipped with diverse weapons, and ordered to kill
each other. There could only be one winner. If, at the
end of three days, more than one student remained
living, the electronic dog collars attached to each child
would explode. Clearly (in case we had somehow
missed the point), it was a dog-eat-dog dystopia that
was intended to ensue.

The video zapped out. The assembled students were busy exuding disbelief and bravado, laughs and chortling sneers, but they abruptly fell silent when their menacing teacher (the iconic Takeshi 'Beat' Kitano) calmly leered, telling them, 'It's your own damn fault. You guys mock grown-ups. Go ahead and mock us.'

Kitano, with the blank unreadability of his thickened neck and hollowed gaze, ploughed the hammy lines with a genuine counterpoint of hazard and dignity. From the first flicker of his heavy-lidded eyes, he possessed the role of demented teacher with uncanny success, and inside the cinema as much as the classroom, a real sense of unease started to thicken around the abstract premise.

On screen, one of the students protested bravely (*you'llnevergetawaywiththis*, she told him). Casually, Kitano aimed and then shot her in the head. She reeled back and then collapsed, dead on arrival. He grinned. The audience murmured appreciatively.

'They're getting into it,' I whispered.

'Very much so.'

The children were dropped onto the island. Predictably, a peacenik contingent emerged; predictably, the peacenik contingent was mowed down by the more brutally disposed schoolchildren. The film was an unruly combination of horror, action, comedy and romance, with a generous slug of graphic violence stirred into the mix. The violence paired up with every genre aspect of the film in a show of consistency that had to be admired, resulting in a staggering series of couplings, reeled off in galloping haste: violent-horror, violent-action, violent-comedy, violent-romance, even, improbable as it sounded, violent-romantic-comedy. But most salient was the film's gleefully stylish aesthetic. Exceptionally good-looking teenage girls panted across the island in short skirts, severing heads with swinging machetes or disembowelling wayward suitors. Boys with bandannas and trendy haircuts gunned down other students while screaming expletives and slogans. It was a point that anybody fat or ugly got killed off very quickly.

Nobody in the audience appeared to lament this discriminatory homicide. When a particularly sexy girl was killed, the audience shifted discontentedly. Somebody booed.

Strictly speaking, the film was about juvenile apathy,

teenage delinquency and violence. But in reality, the film was about the adults. The adults who reacted in fear and hysteria, the adults in their hollow sadism – the adults in their dogged, inexplicable absence. The entire film, with its mad, schizoid energy, was in a sense a fantasia composed by those guilty, absented adults. And that fantasy was not, 'Send any teenager who has ever mouthed off to you to a deserted island where they will be brutally hacked to pieces by another teenager who has mouthed off to you' – but, rather, 'Send your own kids to a deserted island where they will be brutally hacked to pieces by their best friends.'

And that was the crux of the film. Rather than a dystopia on delinquency and the increasing violence of means, the film was a staggeringly effective set piece based on the disjunction between two generations. It was a film, simply and most poignantly, about a generational gap, into which a great many plot twists and severed heads had space to fall. And that gap was grounded not in an abstract future, but rather in the quickly receding present. Everything apart from the actual deserted island frolics, everything in the framing and the establishment of the film's premise, took place in a recognizable Japanese society. The generational gap, with its spreading web of confusion and miscommunication, was finally – or so at least the film seemed to say – the problem at the heart of the current conflict in Japan. It was as prosaic as a growing spread of years.

As it emerged from the cinema, the audience was enthusiastic, if somewhat dazed. I turned to my friend. 'What did you think?'

He shrugged. 'Slightly B-movie. Cult classic, I would imagine. You know – you can practically see the online fansites and the chatrooms. Thousands of geeky kids with *Battle Royale* posters hanging in their bedrooms.'

We looked to one side of the lobby. From a folding table, churlish cinema staff were selling *Battle Royale* posters. A knot of people had already formed around the table. A voice asked if there were T-shirts available for sale. After a momentary pause, it asked why not.

I frowned. 'And they're not even kids.'

'As a film? I don't know. Stylish, cool – all of that. Very hammy, though.'

'I don't mind the melodrama.'

'No, it's odd to complain about the melodrama when the whole film is completely over the top. Cute

47

girls, though, right? That's what everybody cares about.'

He crumpled a plastic water bottle and chucked it towards a rubbish bin. He missed, and it landed somewhere near my left foot. Sighing, I leaned over to pick it up and dropped it into the bin.

'Have you noticed how lately everything Japanese is cool? Clothes, magazines, movies – stuffed animals even.' I paused. 'But there is such a thing as too cool, isn't there?'

I thought there was. The enduring point about *Battle Royale* was that its chic melding of desperation and cool was entirely symptomatic of Japanese youth culture. The underside of its perfect cool gave way to a mire of unforgiving facts: a dramatic rise in violent crime, the spread of panic attacks among the young, grade-school children hooked on anti-depressants, outbreaks of anorexia and bulimia, teenagers holed up in their bedrooms for weeks at a time, students boycotting school and children boycotting life, weird and wondrous stories of stringent denial and fathomless apathy. Yet these facts seemed to pose no direct challenge to the implacable smoothness of the generation's style and flair. Instead, the removed chilliness of cool, the reckless vacancy of casual ennui, was somehow indistinguishable from the psychological paralysis sweeping across the generation. Their cool was, for the less extreme of them, the bedroom into which they retreated. And they seemed, even as you watched, to withdraw into the sanctuary of that cool. They baulked; they backed up; they disappeared into the details of that immaculately rendered surface.

They left behind nothing more than the empty outline of the clothes they wore, as lonely as a room recently vacated. The secret pattern of the place to which they disappeared remained unknown, and ultimately that surface fragmented when pressed too closely. It bowed, it shattered, it let expectation sink to the ground. And the collapse of what was once absolute and impermeable could only leave this generation adrift and abandoned, caught in the aftermath of an unnamed disaster.

The rain slackens and turns instead to a time several years after that rainy walk in London and some short few months before this present visit and this present rain, when Japan was in the midst of what was maybe the longest summer I could remember. I was there on my summer holiday, visiting my parents and working half-heartedly on my doctoral research. I could almost watch as the arguments of my thesis seemed to loosen with the heat; outside, the pavement was too hot to touch, and mothers warned their children to wear shoes when they went out to play. During the day the air was stagnant, and evening brought no respite. Windows and doors were left flung open, and electric fans bladed their way through the night-thickened air.

The facts themselves were nothing much. One child dead, killed by another child, in the incongruous setting of a Japanese grade-school classroom. Had it happened in America, in a post-Columbine landscape, the story would have been familiar enough: the same protagonists, the same antagonists, the same location and the same plot, variation on a theme too common to carry any import of shock or menace. But in Japan the story was received in a different manner. It became – not itself, not the concrete facts of a dead child, a father in mourning and the blankness of all cruelty, but instead the harbinger of a quickly growing generation that was little understood. It became a symbol and it delineated a threshold, teetering on the brink between the comforts of a manageable past, and a future utterly unknown and uncontrollable.

It was in the suffocating claustrophobia of that heat that the case ran with such terrifying speed. The facts, when first we read about them in the newspaper, seemed strangely blank. A twelve-year-old girl had been murdered at school by her eleven-year-old class-mate. There was no explanation of motive or method, no embellishment upon these bone-dry facts, nothing to mitigate or make sense of their baldness. For a day or two the case floated across the fronts of newspapers, empty and insubstantial, but carrying its summertime stench of decay. Aged facts, and no new news; it was the continued and unalleviated blankness that made those facts so offensive and so unbearable, hinting as it did at a kind of senselessness we were unprepared to face.

Then, over the course of a slow week, further details emerged. The newspapers and television news reports told us that the girl had been murdered with a cutting edge, the sort that are used in grade school for arts and crafts courses. A solemn news reporter with a thick middle parting and a canine look of entreaty about the eyes told us that the two girls had been friends. On another channel a young woman with bouffant hair told us that the girl had been found dead in an empty classroom, killed by a 'sharp' instrument of some kind. A syndicated columnist, a middle-aged woman with a fuzzy byline photo, told us that the two girls had quarrelled in an online chatroom – a childish, girlish quarrel, with the murdered girl calling the murderer 'fat'. Of all the facts, most disturbing was the unfathomable childishness of the motive. We somehow knew then that we were not dealing with an adult murderer shrunken into a child's body, but a child murderer, with a child's own reasons and reasonings.

My mom in particular was preoccupied with the case, though the concrete reasons for that preoccupation eluded us. She was the one who brought us updates on the investigation, gleaned from daily papers and television news reports, from op-ed pieces in weekly magazines; she was the one who worried over it and watched for it, bringing it up in conversation so regularly that it soon took on the strange familiarity of a mantra. Daily, over the course of a summer month, she brought the case to our doorstep and into our home.

'Look,' my mom said one morning; on one such day.

She spoke across a cluttered breakfast table. Tea and coffee cups, thick slices of toast and jam, a glass container holding butter, boxes of cereal and cartons of yogurt were scattered across the tablecloth. Sections of three newspapers – two Japanese and one English language – were portioned out around the table, and we were, as per custom, quiet behind these newsprint barriers, reading in privacy as we ate our breakfast. The family dog travelled round the table, wearing a sheepishly determined expression as he begged for scraps.

'Look,' she repeated.

She folded a page of the paper back upon itself, and cleared her throat. My dad lowered his newspaper a fraction of an inch. The top of his head tilted to one side, in a gesture of acquiescence running tight on a timer. I continued reading my paper.

'*The perpetrator's teachers considered her a well-adjusted student. She excelled in her studies, and was always respect-ful and well-behaved, though some recall she was at times a little withdrawn.'*

'Hmm.' After a civil pause, the sheath of newsprint moved back upwards, and the circumference of my dad's head disappeared from view.

'Who? Whose teachers?' I asked.

'The girl who murdered that other girl.'

'Oh.' I paused. The dog whined faintly, nudging at my leg with his nose. Although I was only an occasional visitor, he had me remembered as a soft touch. I lowered my paper and patted him on the nose. He grinned a little with his eyes. Then, shifting his weight, he prodded my leg again.

I looked at my mom.

'You mean, respectful and well-behaved when she wasn't killing other girls?'

'Oh, wait. *The other children in the class, however, describe the perpetrator as a bully, recollecting that she would often get angry and violent for no reason –*'

'Well, there you go. That sounds more like it.'

'*– but claim she concealed that side of her personality from adults.*'

The dog whined again. I fed him a piece of toast.

'Drink your coffee,' my dad intoned from behind his newspaper. 'It's getting cold.' My mom ignored him and continued reading.

'. . . *the perpetrator was known to have read extensively, in particular violent horror novels and mystery books . . .*'

'What does that mean?'

'I'm not sure.'

'I read a lot of mystery books when I was little. *You* read a lot of mystery books. You still do.'

'I suppose,' my dad said mildly, 'it somehow feels better if there are reasons, however silly those reasons might be.' He sighed and lowered his newspaper, submitting to the necessity of conversation. He peered dolefully into his cup, then reached for the sugar.

'How do you mean?'

'It's natural to look for explanations. To say that it's because she read horror books, or mystery books, or whatever it is. There's great comfort in cause and effect.'

'They've been doing psychological profiling,' my mom said doubtfully.

'And?'

'Well, they don't know yet. But they say the girl is very pretty,' my mom added vaguely. She paused. 'Oh. They've found out more about how the actual murder took place.' She leaned in closer to the page. *'During a school recess, the perpetrator lured the victim to an empty classroom, and under the pretence of playing a game, blindfolded and tied the girl.'* I put down my toast. The dog's eyes brightened hopefully, and he wagged his tail politely. *'Initially the victim cooperated, but soon began struggling and asking to be released. It is believed that the perpetrator then slit her throat with a razor edge.'*

'God.'

I fed the dog the toast.

'There's not butter on that toast, is there?' My mom looked at me. 'Because you know butter is so bad for him.' Looking back down at the paper, she cleared her throat. *'The perpetrator waited until she was certain the victim was dead, then returned to her classroom. According to her teacher, the perpetrator's uniform was covered in blood, and she was very calm. She told the teacher where to find the body, and later claimed to have planned the murder several days in advance.'*

She lowered the newspaper with a sigh. 'Well.' Her

eyes fell on the dog. He was licking at his chops in a spasm of enthusiasm. She frowned.

'No more human food for you, young man.'

'Young dog.'

'Young *dog* –'

'Why are you so preoccupied with this murder case?' my dad asked.

My mom put down her paper, and looked at my dad. 'I don't know.' She took a sip of her coffee, then replaced the cup in its saucer. 'It's just that they're so young,' she said, her voice straining in mild protest. 'And there's something so unfathomable about this girl. She had her parents, her teachers, she had all the adults around her completely fooled. The other children were on to her, but the adults – the adults had no idea.'

'The adults were maybe not paying close enough attention,' my dad said. 'Children learn a code very early on, about how their behaviour is read—'

'And the fact of the matter is,' my mom continued, ignoring him, 'we know nothing about this generation. They're unmotivated, they're surly and lazy, they seem desperately unhappy and we don't know what's making them act this way. They're a mystery. The adults around them, their own parents, don't understand them at all. You hear stories nowadays that are incredible.' She paused, collecting her thoughts. 'This case has only highlighted something that has been growing for some time now. An attitude of fear.'

'You're absolutely right there. It's a culture of fear,' my dad said. 'And the worst thing about a culture of fear is that it gathers momentum as you talk about it, in the media, in the family, at the breakfast table, as we're doing now. It becomes unstoppable. It contaminates everything.' He put his hands down on the table emphatically, suddenly irate.

The dog burped, then looked at me with a guilty expression. My dad looked at the dog, then looked at me.

'Could you please stop feeding the dog from the table?'

'I'm not feeding him anything,' I protested.

'I saw you slip him more toast.'

'Yes – you're always feeding the dog. And you *know* how bad human food is for him.'

'I don't even have any toast on my plate.'

'That's because you gave it all to him. I've been watching. You've hardly eaten anything yourself – you never eat proper food. Really, I shudder to think how you eat when you're in London.'

'I can cook, kind of . . .'

'Whatever. The point is that whenever you're here, you feed the dog human food and he gets terrible indigestion from it, and then he doesn't want to eat his dog food any more, and you know very well that we especially picked the organic macrobiotic science diet for him, we're very strict—'

'What's wrong with you guys? Why are you so irritable all of a sudden? It's not like *I* killed anybody.'

'I'm not irritable. I'm not irritable at all,' my dad said. 'I just want to get back to reading about this proposed lightrail system in São Paulo,' he said in a superior tone. 'It's a fascinating article. All about user behaviour patterns and decision making.'

'Fascinating.'

'Now there's no reason to be disrespectful about your father's interests, just because we caught you feeding the dog – caught you red-handed I might add . . .'

That evening, my mom and I went by bus to a local restaurant where we were meeting some family friends for dinner. It was getting on for six o'clock, an hour when the bus is always loud with the tangential chatter of schoolchildren, business people discussing cases and clients, friends loping their way through a good recapitulation. It was still light, and as people stepped from the blustery heat outside into the air-conditioned coolness of the bus, they shivered at the plunge in temperature and wiped at the sweat on their foreheads and necks.

Two young women in pastel suits sat near the back. Their hair was sleekly trimmed, their noses powdered, and severely masculine briefcases rested at their feet. They were talking animatedly; one of them said something, leaning forward slightly and covering her mouth as she spoke, and then they both laughed. In front of them sat an old man with a double seat to himself and no visible intention of sharing. He had his hands propped on his walking stick and was somewhere between asleep and awake, uttering loud guttural sounds as he breathed. Three middle-aged ladies were sitting in the seats adjacent, a cacophonous chorus of gossiping; a young man in headphones and a suit fitting awkwardly at the shoulders stood in front of them, hand looped through one of the vinyl handles hanging from the ceiling. He moved uncomfortably, looking to one side, then turned up the volume on his disc player.

The bus slowed to a stop, and a cluster of uniformed schoolgirls clambered noisily aboard. There were four, perhaps five of them, and they gave a mixed impression of hair in bangs and bobs and thick ponytails, scuffed knees and hairless legs. Their sneakers squeaked on the vinyl flooring of the bus, and their cheeks were flushed. Dampness touched upon lithe, athletic bodies, and they looked as though they were returning home from a spirited sports practice of some kind.

They created an impression, in the rawness of their vigorous youth, in the clumsiness of self-consciousness not yet fitted to size and the dense imprecision of their movements – in their approximate resemblance to the schoolgirls we had recently been seeing everywhere in the news. A jumbled assortment of wide eyes, gaping smiles, full lips and black hair, they were a parody of schoolgirls in their navy pleated uniforms, and they seemed to carry with them a dash of lately associated recklessness.

Large clusters of keyrings and mascots – Winnie the Pooh clutching a pot of honey, Minnie Mouse in her red-spotted dress – hung from the oversize sports bags casually slung over their shoulders, and as they moved, bags swinging and knees working, keyrings flying, the bus grew suddenly full. In a moment the collective noise escalated several notches; with a sigh, the pastel women gave up on their conversation and folded their hands resignedly. The young man with the headphones looked at the girls, then turned up the volume on his disc player until it hit maximum. The old man remained enveloped in the cloud of his semi-somnolence, walking stick jolting from side to side. Slowly, the windows of the bus fogged with steam.

One of the girls was standing at the edge of the group, back hunched against their merriment. She bore the same residue of exertion as the other girls, but here that dampness was somehow vaguely unhealthy. Her calves, massively overdeveloped, protruded beneath knock-knees, setting her body visibly off-balance. Her upper torso ran to the surprising counterpoint of a sunken delicacy, so that everything looked out of proportion and showed signs of a subtle malfunctioning. Her uniform was stained and wrinkled, her hair unkempt, and she wore her skirt several inches too high. Winnie the Pooh and Minnie Mouse hung hopefully from her bag, velour matted and features worn.

The other girls pointedly ignored her, back turned against back. From that locked perimeter, their muffled conversation rose and fell in the exaggerated rhythms of teenage banter: intimate whispers, tones of inflated surprise, jeers of puncturing harshness. One of them laughed, a trilling sound that carried and bounced off the sides of the bus before slowing into a sneer.

A middle-aged woman reached down to massage her calf, voice complaining. The girl rubbed at her nose. With a sudden and powerful roll of the shoulders, the strap of her bag was dislodged – a faint vapour of helpless malice flashed into the air – the bag crashed to the ground with surprising force, cutting off the woman's meandering grievance. Its falling edge narrowly missed the sleeping old man, who woke with a start; as it hit the ground, falling amidst a crowd of feet, the floor of the bus trembled with nervous vibrations. Several people turned to look in the girl's direction, and the middle-aged woman froze, hand on leg.

The girl slouched back into stillness. Hulking awkwardly, bag resting at her feet, she seemed impervious to the stares of the other passengers. She rubbed at her nose again.

As the bus approached its next stop, a passenger brushed by, struggling towards the doors at the front. The girl turned round, body lurching back into powerful motion. This time, the sharp point of her elbow clipped the young man with the headphones. Warily, he moved several feet away, whereupon she glared at him through the overhang of her hair. He stopped, nervous and uncertain. A distant hush fell over the bus. The other girls turned their heads to look, strangely quiet; glances were exchanged among the passengers.

She got off a few stops later with the other girls. A palpable release shot through the bus when she stepped off, and for a moment the passengers indulged in their shared relief. An air of near jollity seemed to pass between them; the middle-aged woman mouthed,

'Phew!' to my mom, who smiled and shook her head ruefully; the old man nodded sagely to the young man with headphones, who looked down uncertainly. I turned my head to look through the window as the bus lurched forward again. The other girls had linked arms and pulled ahead, skirts flying and lips pulled back in laughter. The girl trailed behind, legs working clumsily, then stopped and shifted her bag from shoulder to shoulder.

My mom leaned towards me. 'You can just tell, they were all looking at that girl, and wondering . . .'

'She was just awkward.'

'Maybe. But there was something strange about her. You know. The way she was swinging her bag around, and the way her hair hung over her face.' Her voice was excited.

It was true. There had been more to her than awkwardness.

'You could tell,' my mom persisted, 'you could tell that's what everybody was thinking. You could practically see the thought running through their head.'

'I know. I agree.'

'People are scared of little girls in uniforms now.'

'Yes – but rationally speaking, if for every psycho-path there are several million perfectly normal adolescent girls, you have to admit that the odds are mostly in favour of the perfectly normal girls.'

'But remember how after Columbine everybody was terrified of those teenage boys in trench coats? They couldn't help it. Even if they knew that five years later the majority of those boys would end up married with kids, they still couldn't help it. It wasn't a question of rational thinking. It was beyond that.'

'The next stop is us,' she said suddenly. She got up, then began walking unevenly down the aisle. I followed her.

'Well,' I said as we stepped off the bus, 'it's a generational gap, isn't it? It happens everywhere. Japan isn't the only place where parents don't get the kind of music their children listen to.'

'Yes, but it's more serious in Japan, because here families are more dependent on each other. The generations are pressed closer together. In America, when you turn sixteen, you get a car; when you turn eighteen, you move out of the house – twenty-one and you're independent. It's not like that here. Children live at home well into their twenties. In many cases they live at home until, or even after, they get married. So if parents and children don't get along, it's serious. It's a problem.'

We turned into a narrow side street. An apartment block stretched down the street. I peered up at the endless rows of short balconies and small double-glazed windows. Limp shirts and socks were pegged onto washing lines and mats aired over railings, giving a shabby intimacy to the place. On the other side of the street, several darkened *machiya* houses rested still and close to the ground.

'What are you doing?'

I turned. My mom was standing several paces ahead, looking back at me. 'Nothing,' I said, and hurried to catch up.

'Anyway,' she continued, 'houses are so small in Japan . . .' She paused, her eyes scanning the buildings around us. 'I can't quite remember where the restaurant is,' she murmured.

'Go on,' I said.

'What? Oh,' she said. 'Well, the houses are so small,

and when you get two or three, sometimes even four, generations living in a single home – you need a strong sense of family to survive that. But nowadays, no family has that strong a relationship. That kind of relationship itself doesn't exist any more.'

'What happens then?'

'I don't know. People get used to living together like strangers. People get used to not knowing each other. But I almost think it's better to hate your parents, or hate your children, than not know them at all.'

I thought about the Japanese homes I had been in – small airless apartments, tiny houses with closed-off rooms. The contents were often of the same diminished architecture, small bedrooms with shallow wardrobes and a narrow perimeter rimming a twin bed; a single bathroom overflowing with the assorted mess of shampoo bottles, hand mirrors and tweezers, face wash, moisturizers, hair tonic, acne cream, the collected grooming implements of an entire nuclear family squeezed into an insufficient number of bathroom cabinets; a combination living/dining/family room with a miniature kitchen appended, a multi-purpose space where the noise of the television contended with the murmur of conversation and a small and crazed dog chased its tail; sandbox rooms with transparent acoustics linked together by the narrowest of corridors. These houses and these rooms could not help but breed the contagion of misconstruction that sprang from claustrophobia. There was not enough space to live like strangers.

A flock of teenage boys on bicycles turned off the main road and came swooping down the narrow street. I turned my head; a coarse eruption of laughter twanged wide through the air. There were maybe five or six of them. They flew across the pavement, bicycles leaping through uneven patches of light, voices rough and loud. As they came swarming towards us, I could see that they were sloppily dressed in their school uniforms, shirts untucked and shoelaces untied. Their backs were hunched and their heads pushed down as they pedalled towards us on their bicycles. Intuitively, my spine stiffened. I looked at my mom. Her lips were pressed together and she was striding ahead firmly.

Another moment and they were upon us. I saw a flash of silver chain; a low and vulgar laugh; a dyed head of hair flying past; an almost canine grin and open mouth. A whirr of wheel, a metal gear in flux. I jumped, and clutched at my bag. A moment later and they had sped past, already receding from sight. My heart thumped and I was short of breath. Embarrassed, I blushed. My mom smiled.

'They're just kids on bikes,' she said. 'Nothing to be afraid of.'

'I know, but I'm feeling kind of jumpy.'

Her face lit up as we came to a stop before a small restaurant. A light outside glowed cosily. 'Ah, found it. Here it is.' She paused as she opened the door. 'Come on, we're late.' She stepped inside as I held the door open. Distantly, I heard her greet some friends. '. . . I know, it's been too long . . .'

I turned my head to look down the street, but it was empty and still.

I wake up when the train makes a brief stop at some undisclosed location, one that remains undisclosed, the haziness of my waking continuing beyond the stop, beyond the passing of the signs that reveal the still hidden name of the station and into the train's smooth resumption of speed.

And when, more fully awake, I look up again, I see that the train is inside Tokyo, and that the city has leapt upon and swallowed us unawares. The glitter and flash of the city's lights – those lights that never shut off, only fade blinking into daylight and then re-emerge again come dusk – once so distant, are now suddenly close. They are pressed against the glass of the train windows, their colours and shapes blurring through the recurring rain, and as we finally arrive in Tokyo, it is as though the train has been freshly doused in the wash of the city.

Around me passengers start to gather their things. A businessman stands, yawning, and wrenches his briefcase up from the floor with a sharp snap of the arm; a young mother coaxes her son into a winter hat and gloves before retreating down the aisle and towards the carriage doors.

I pull on my coat and hoist my bag down, then join them.

20 March 1995, 7.52 a.m.

It started with a cough, a slow coughing that was no different from an ordinary cough – a spot of dust caught in the throat, the lingering residue of a winter cold – and that spread its way down the spine of the subway commuter train, leaping lightly from carriage to carriage.

It crept past a young woman in a pale-green suit, who leaned forward, hand on chest, briefcase slipping from stockinged knees. It hurtled forward several hundred feet to an elderly man, who looked up and blinked, then removed his glasses to rub his eyes. Airborne, moving on the draught that blew through the carriages, it rapidly skimmed across the edge of a newspaper before pausing to linger round a sleeping construction worker. Then, it swept downwards and ducked into the open air-vents that connected the carriages.

After that, it was everywhere, and the whole train was coughing. Fingers clutching at handkerchiefs, hands spread over mouths, a unanimous chorus of spluttering that ran the length of the Marunouchi Line. As the train sped from Ochanomizu Station towards Ogikubo, the carriages rocked uneasily. Slowly, a heavy smell of sweetness began to spread through the air. As the passengers looked up, constriction knocked hard upon their chests, and their breath grew short as the air around them ran dry. Then the darkness of the subway became more pervasive, as pupils contracted and the radius of available light rapidly diminished.

By the time the train stopped at Nakano-sakakue Station, passengers were bursting from the carriages and two people – a man and a woman – had collapsed, foaming at the mouth. The foam was of a pinkish tint, stained with blood, and they looked, sprawled lonely on the ground, like the victims of an ill-conceived suicide pact. Between them lay a crumpled newspaper – the soiled pages of a sports tabloid, words and images blotted out by a sticky liquid substance – from which seeped a puddle that slowly spread across the floor of the train.

Above ground, the nightmare had deepened. People lay slumped or sprawled across the pavement in temporary shelters. Spoons were propped crooked in their mouths, shivering between chattering teeth and crystallized with specks of foam. Several station workers sat on bordered flowerbeds, heads bowed down, eyes streaming uncontrollably. The sharp smell of crushed leaves mingled with the shallow sound of their breathing. Dazed, fighting back the darkness clouding their vision, ghostly passengers wandered aimless amidst the fallen bodies. Deserted at the end of the world, the gathered group stopped to listen as, one by one, ambulances streaked through the city morning. They heard the wail of sirens come tantalizingly close before fading away into the distance. Then they listened again as the sound of sirens stopped altogether, and lapsed into a second, heavier, silence.

At some point, into that thickened silence, the word

'Aum' was first spoken. At some point the word was released into the air, a sound as gnawed through with darkness as the smell of sarin that had assailed them underground. And as the victims wandered across Tokyo, sight and senses failing, still their minds kept fumbling back to the terrible cult of despair. Moving through a growing darkness, they conjured forth the guilty shaman with his unfathomable powers, the clandestine blindness of a hope-starved elite; as the light faded out, they glimpsed the outline of a national failing grown so acute that it had, that late winter's morning, reached its brutal extremity.

The 1995 Tokyo Gas Attack left twelve people dead and thousands more injured. Responsible for the attack was Aum Shinrikyo, a cult drawn from the elite population of Japan, whose membership included university-trained doctors and scientists. Both the attack and the emergence of Aum Shinrikyo provoked a crisis of doubt in the nation. But what made that doubt speak, at such lengths and so persuasively, was not the spectacular narrative of hijacked despair and hopelessness; not indoctrination's powers of erasure, nor the terror of charisma's dazzle. Rather, it was the dull sense that, on that morning in March, the inevitability of cause and slow consequence had been confirmed.

And of all that had passed, it was simply this that remained: the certainty that the attack was no aberration, but instead the neatly plotted denouement to a game that had, move by slow move, left the Japanese people with fewer options, and fewer routes of escape.

THE BUBBLE

Place: Osaka, Japan

When a bullet train hits its terminal velocity, it moves so quickly that the view from the window dissolves into patches of vertigo. The pacing of its superhuman straining inserts a wedge between the blurred landscape outside and the buoyant stillness inside the carriage; once a bullet train hits its stride, it is better to abandon the view through the glass and settle into your seat, into your book or thoughts – or your *bento* boxed meal. It is only when the train is in approach or when the train is pulling away that the view outside will settle, palm in palm, with the movement of the train; only then will you suddenly again feel that a journey is being undertaken.

Several days after my arrival in Japan, I ride the bullet train westwards from Tokyo to Osaka. The last few days have passed with the fleet rapidity lent by pleasure, for there is always an undisclosed pleasure in returning to Japan, one that, however much anticipated, still lends small, regular shocks of surprise; that is to be found in the details of sundry sun-drenched events: a sip of sweet Royal Milk Tea, can plundered from a nearby vending machine; the slow swing open of an automated taxi door; the affectionate abbreviation of my Japanese middle name, *Megumi* becoming *Megu-chan*, *Megu-kun*, these substitute namings rushing towards me in the showering of a warm and impetuous colloquy, as though the syllables had for a moment been held still in the mouth, before being suddenly released. But, for all these incidental pleasures, I am nonetheless anxious to arrive at my parents' home, which is simply another way of saying that I am anxious to see my father.

The seeing is important, irreplaceable, for the evidence of my eyes will confirm the truth of his recovery – recovery at times seeming like a promise too easily

broken, a cover designed to disguise the hard straining
of two opposing vectors, the bettering of recovery
being set against, and also a part of, an opposing pull,
in an opposing direction. And so once the bullet train
pulls away from the station, the figure of my cousin –
waving blithely before turning to trip away down the
platform – receding with accelerating rapidity, I am
happy, if not to be leaving Tokyo, then to be heading
towards Osaka.

The two cities, placed at the centre of two Japans,
Western and Eastern, might be said to represent oppos-
ing tendencies. As I make this journey I am abruptly
reminded that my mother comes from the East, my
father from the West, and that, even when they are
meeting in the middle, there is still a multitude of
small differences between them. And if, as the train
pulls out of Tokyo Station, I am in a sense leaving the
birthplace of my mother, then – the vertical assem-
blage of buildings and lights flying into the distance
and the train heading towards the more solid sprawl
of Osaka – I am also in a sense returning to a place
long familiar to my father.

There can be something of the dream to Tokyo,

but Osaka has a ready-hewn roughness that is equally compelling. Much of the country's commerce and industry is housed in Osaka, which plays metaphorical host to the still powerful ambition surging out of Japan (and surely it is significant that this bullet train, so much a symbol of Japanese technological achievement, so much a vehicle destined for the future, is presently moving away from Tokyo, and towards Osaka). The city is touched with the residue of a greater ambition that, not too long ago, coupled with the famed Japanese work ethic to engender the buoyant economy of the Eighties. And I realize, sitting aboard this bullet train bound for Osaka, that I have never been entirely able to divorce the weight of that work ethic from the cancer that overcame my father, so that they are all bound up together: the hurtling forward of the train, the characters spelled out upon its destination placard, the reasons for my being here, on this particular train, at this particular time.

I carry in my wallet a photograph of my dad and two of his best friends, placed there during what were for me the more worrying days of his recurring illness (those days when I was in London and he was somewhere in Japan, lying in an anonymous and unseen hospital bed; days when I was unable to concentrate and instead spent long hours ploughing through books without reading anything at all). In the photo he sits with his friends at a restaurant dinner table. They are smiling for the camera, just three middle-aged men enjoying a meal. They gaze into the lens with the mitigated naturalness of artificially posed photographs – a little code of artifice so instantly recognized and read that it has acquired its own special aura of naturalness, and it is easy to imagine life's continuum beyond the edges of the image.

The picture is framed and composed with the careful precision of the amateur: the figures centred with the mechanical caution of the viewfinder, the image wrought in the impersonal sharpness of autofocus. The real personality of the picture, the intrepidity of the eager amateur, only declares itself in the evidence of technical imperfections that threaten to mar the image. The flash has broken out overstrong, so that the details of their features bleed into celestial flatness while everything else in the image is plunged into indeterminate darkness. Off to one side, the waitress is faintly discernible as a sliver of white sleeve, blurred with motion.

My dad is sitting in the middle, looking much the California academic despite the ten years that have passed since his return to Japan. He always looks still in photographs, which can give him an air of shy, benevolent certainty. While those around him radiate fidgety impatience, brittleness or breathless exuberance (a whole series of infinitesimal movements, instantly seized by the lens and converted into so many pixels, embedded into so many millimetres of negative), he always remains motionless, radiating the unwearied patience of his smile. In pictures he has the smile of a child, though that smile is rarely his in real life.

Mr T sits to one side, leaning forward towards the camera. His posture makes him look a size larger than my dad, hulking to one side protectively, but in reality they are the same size and height. Mr T has acquired a trim, sturdy figure from long weekend hikes. He and his wife regularly hike to distant temples and shrines in the Kansai region of Japan, through woods and over mountains, mutually indifferent to rain and sunshine.

His hair is still black and thick enough, but not so thick as to render careful brushing and arrangement entirely redundant. He has a friendly face, and he tucks in the corners of his mouth as he gazes into the camera.

Mr T is your typical bureaucrat. He lives in a nice house in a prestigious neighbourhood of Kyoto. His wife is youthful and beautiful and in many other ways perfect; his daughter is pretty and graceful and attends one of the elite women's colleges in Kyoto; his son is surprisingly tall and in his first year at an esteemed university; they own two expensive and fluffy thoroughbred cats that pretty much have the run of the house. Every day he commutes over an hour and a half to Osaka, where he works for the city government. He is one of the hundreds of conservatively clad businessmen that can be seen on any given day, riding the train in the early hours of the morning and returning late in the evening. He has worked as a civil servant the whole of his professional life, and will continue to work for another seven or eight years before settling into a comfortable retirement, serviced by an excellent pension. By then, what little remains outstanding on his mortgage will be paid off, his children will be settled, and he and his family will be able to spend leisurely weekends at their second home in the mountains. His hobbies, which he pursues with keen passion, include photography and hiking.

In the picture Mr T is staring intently at the camera, which is some feet away, perched on a tripod and working on a timer. The camera is his, which maybe explains some of the anxiety in his eyes. They have been sitting, posed and waiting, for what seems an inordinately long time. He worries that the timer has grown temperamental; perhaps the battery has run out of juice; perhaps he forgot to press the start button, that has happened before. His smile is a little pinched because of those multiple anxieties, the corners tucked in deeper than usual, and behind his glasses, his eyes are round with doubtful anticipation. To his relief, the camera finally gives a slow whirr followed by a bright flash and a delightfully audible click. For a moment all three of them – Mr T, my dad, and Mr S – remain frozen in place, mutely staring at the little black contraption on its spindly legs.

'Just one more!' Mr T says, and he stands up and hurries over to the tripod. Mr S rolls his eyes with a sarcastic grimace, reaching for a glass; my dad takes off his glasses to rub away the after-effect of the flash. The waitress comes to the table with a tray bearing coffees and plated desserts. Mr T bends close to the camera, glasses resting on his forehead and eyes squinting at the viewfinder. 'Could we get another bottle of wine?' Mr S says under his breath to the waitress. He looks at the dessert plate set before him. 'Hey! What is this again?'

My dad stirs his camomile tea. He fishes out the teabag with two fingers and a spoon. Blinking, he sips sedately.

'Excuse me,' Mr T says as he squeezes past the waitress and hurries back to his place. 'OK, here we go,' he says to himself, and gazes towards the camera with the same anxious expression as before. My dad reiterates his still, secret smile; Mr S gulps down the last dregs of wine in his glass, craning his neck to see where the waitress has gone. He puffs at his cigarette, then pulls it away in time to grin for the camera as the bulb flashes.

Mr S lies at the opposite end of the spectrum from Mr T. In the photograph, he sits with his head drawn up, as with a sudden gesture, and smiles with toothy unevenness. There is the trace of a rambunctious leer in his smile, and it is easy to glimpse his younger self peeping through. He smokes and drinks and indulges in rich foods without compunction. In the happy inebriation of his more expansive moments, he insists that he'll be the first to teeter off towards death, but in reality he typifies the meaning of the phrase 'rude health'.

Mr S is an eccentric, particularly in the context of Japanese society. He is what might, at one time, have been called a bon vivant. He throngs his life with pleasures – with the slow-moving leisure of idleness, the aesthetic pleasures of excellent clothes, the sensual delights of good food and drink. The fundamental pursuit of his life is no more or less complicated than the chasing of whim. He stalks the course of his whim with the obsession of the connoisseur, hounding it through the leaps and starts of a garrulous spontaneity, travelling from slum to teahouse with equal ease.

'He only does what he wants,' my dad once explained. 'That is the thing about S.' He paused, then continued in a voice that was half wondering. 'If you stop to think about it,' he said, 'it's kind of amazing, isn't it?' Mr S always means what he says and always means what he does – that's why, I think, my dad calls him 'amazing'. It has always been a revelation to my father that some part of him is both puzzled and moved by what can only be termed a kind of old-fashioned concern with morals.

I look up through the window. Outside, as the train shoots through the outskirts of Tokyo, the build-up of glass and steel dissolves into erratic low rises and listless suburban sprawl. Moving through this thinning landscape, the scenery outside slows and then momentarily falls into the eye's grasp. And though it is only that the rate of movement has grown harder to measure, the landscape outside having so quickly lost its density, it seems almost as though the train has stayed its acceleration, simply that it might accommodate the framing of the view outside.

Slowly now, the train passes a cluster of farm fields, patches of neatly bordered green tended by solitary farmhouses. They are spread out as a constellation, connected to each other by thin streams of road, and at their centre squats a large brown building. Though it doesn't stand very tall, it seems to loom over the surrounding landscape. Erected across its front are the neon *katakana* characters reading PA-CHI-N-KO, and the sight of those letters immediately recollects Mr S – a leisure gambler and a casual frequenter of Pachinko parlours – so that the landscape outside seems to fold and fall back into the recently recollected photograph, tucked back inside my wallet. Instinctively, I move a hand to touch my bag, and then, reassured, return to the slow view from the window.

The Pachinko parlour is still in the midst of its slackened approach. And the longer I look, the more convincingly does the building, with the insistent legibility of its flashing letters, appear like a squared pyramid, a Mecca of calculated risk. There are no other public buildings visible – no supermarket, no drug store, not even a bar or restaurant – and I notice that all the narrowed roads of that cluster (it is not even a village, it is nothing more than a handful of cultivated fields and houses resting alongside the train tracks) lead directly to the parlour. Here all roads point not to Rome, but to Pachinko. A moment later, acceleration resumes, and the whole picture, the fragile constellation, falls apart, sliding past the frame of the window.

Pachinko is a game of joyless excess. It is the kind of game that, once begun, one is likely to get stuck on. It is too easy to while away an unknown count of hours inside these parlours, whose fluorescent-lit interiors betray no evidence of the quickly passing day outside. It is too easy to get caught up in the bland hopefulness of the game, that the big jackpot is always about to descend, the lucky break just around the corner. Pachinko is underwritten by the logic of excess, and there is a definite, deliberate ethos of multiplication at work here – in the shower of little silver balls constantly flying across the monitor, in the incessant stream of bells and whistles ringing out, in the hysteria of sound and movement and psychology, impossible to track or trace.

Pachinko is like a hybrid of pinball and slot machines. A spurt of silver balls shoots out from one side of the machine. The player directs the balls towards a kind of jackpot hole, which subsequently sets off a slot machine mechanism. Should the icons arrange themselves properly, a shoal of little silver balls comes bursting out from the bottom of the machine. In the smaller parlours the traditional icons of assorted fruits spin round joylessly; in the newer parlours everything from rounds of sushi (cartoonishly unappetizing pieces of *ika*, *maguro*, *unagi*, *kappa*, spinning round on plates) to sea creatures (squid, dolphins, turtles, even mermaids, swimming through watery landscapes) declares the nature of your fortune.

Built into the logic of the game is the pretence of a nominal skill requirement, which lures customers into believing that they can become 'better' at playing. But mostly it is a matter of logging time and waiting for the head of luck to strike. Customers perch before the machines for hours, in a state of near paralysis. Here there is none of the enthusiasm, the excitement, that you can sometimes feel in a casino in Las Vegas, or Reno, or Atlantic City – the excited tourists spinning their way through twenty dollars counted out in nickels, the grannies descended on Sin City for a high-school gambling reunion, the Florida condominium-inhabiting couples caught up in the wistful melancholy of a golden anniversary trip – all of which is due to the fact that playing a bit of Pachinko is as common and unremarkable as shopping for groceries, or paying a gas bill. There are very few Pachinko enthusiasts, but there is instead a whole population that plays Pachinko with the casual regularity of the addicted.

Certainly there is something very particular in the way Pachinko hones the player's desire, and whets the gambler's risk. Traditionally the winnings of Pachinko are paid out by a points system; points (awarded according to the number of little silver balls accumulated) are redeemed against everything from Christian Dior handbags, Marlboro cigarettes, bottles of whisky and bottles of soy sauce to toilet paper, children's toys, candy bars and instant microwave meals. These diverse goods are ubiquitous within the parlours, on counters and in Perspex cabinets, so that the object of your desire is always present just before your eyes. Couture handbags and lipsticks dangle in the air, suspended by fishing wire above economy-sized bottles of washing liquid. The juxtaposition is a strange one, not least because of the way it declares the wayward subjectivity of our desire, its flights of fancy and its final prosaic grounds. However much the average Pachinko player may long for the Dior handbag or the

Dunhill wallet, she knows that ultimately she must plunk down her silver balls in exchange for an extra-large package of crackers, a bottle of frying oil, a three-roll pack of paper towels and a five-box pack of Kleenex. The effect is part gambling hall, part low-end department store, part discount supermarket. And it is the constant disappointment of our desire, the hand-bags and the jewellery that are relinquished in favour of a bale of nappies, that lends the place its final tawdriness.

I have – perhaps because there is nonetheless some-thing beguiling in the childish logic of Pachinko barter, something that recollects carnival fairgrounds replete with candy-striped booths, points earned and stuffed animals, boxes of cigarettes and sweets, hardly won – been obsessed with Pachinko parlours since my childhood. I remember the Japan of childhood visits and summertime stays according to the secret incli-nations of that obsession. Whenever I heard the magic word 'Pachinko', my ears would fumble to convert fugitive snatches of Japanese conversation into a more legible English, that I might better retain the imprint of whatever piece of information, whatever tiny detail, had therein been yielded. Walking down the streets of Tokyo or Osaka, I would slow my pace, dawdling a little that I might peer into the parlours. And though the windows were mostly obscured by those opaque *manga*-decorated façades so common to Pachinko parlours, with nothing beyond a few pale whiffs of smoke and the deadening beat of music betraying any hint of what took place inside, I remained transfixed before them.

But of all these juvenile longings tangled up in Japan, the most distinct, the most poignant and resonant, involved that obscure object of desire, the little silvered Pachinko ball. During one of these exercises in dawdling and in what was one of childhood's more blissful moments, I found one of those silver balls on the pavement outside a Pachinko parlour. It was resting in the centre of the pavement, as though it had been dropped unknowingly by an exiting customer, or somehow leapt and rolled its way from one of the machines, down the aisle and out the door. Before my mom could object, I bent down and, pretending to tie my shoelace, slipped the ball into the palm of my hand. I hung onto it for weeks, carrying it in my pocket like a little talisman, my fingers feeling out the smoothness of its surface, the jagged seam that ran round its circumference. Sometimes, in secret, I would bring it out of my pocket and sniff at the bitter pong of its metal.

I continued lingering before Pachinko parlours, hoping against hope to spot the gleam of another wayward silver ball and all the while entertaining fantasies of hoarding enough stray silver balls that I might, eventually and over my young lifetime, trade them in for a plastic tea set, or a teddy bear. (When, several years later and on the cusp of my American adolescence, I came across the silver ball among a drawer of old things, I threw it away. It seemed, in the newly donned perspective of my teenage years, a silly enough thing to keep, and I tossed it into the bin with a resounding *ping*. The moment I threw it away, of course, I regretted it. But it was too late. I heard a distant voice call out, 'Take out the trash, will you? The garbage man will be here any minute.' My teenage brother slouched in and, without a word, slung the binbag over his shoulder and trudged out to deposit it in the bins outside. From inside the house I heard the muffled roar of the rubbish lorry. The door slammed, and my little silver ball was gone for ever.)

Then, many years later when I returned to visit Japan as an adult, Mr S asked if I'd like to go to play some Pachinko. The dust flew off, the fantasy roused itself back to creaking life and I leapt at the unexpected chance of resurrecting an old childhood dream. It is that unanticipated restoration that I remember now, as I relinquish the view outside the train and settle into the state of drowsy wakefulness that to me seems so often to sprawl out from train journeys and partial remembrances, so that there is now a kind of double return, the return of that past adventure, as well as the attendant childhood longing it carries, still lingering close.

He had suggested it lightly, carelessly, over a cup of tea, on one of those regular occasions when my parents and I had travelled to Kyoto for the day (my father there for work purposes, my mother and I for an itinerary of shopping and time-killing leisure no less onerous).

'Oh no,' my mom had said, shaking her head decisively. 'You'll hate it. Terrible places – cigarette smoke and loud music.'

'I don't mind,' I remember saying.

'No, believe me. You won't like it at all. Besides,' she continued, head shaking again, 'the people who play Pachinko really aren't that nice.'

'Meaning people like me?' Mr S asked drily.

My mom looked at him, and smiled despite herself. 'Exactly,' she said. 'The idle and the unemployed. Do you really want to go spend the afternoon in a room with cigarette smoke and loud music and a bunch of people like Mr S?'

'I'm just curious.'

'At least it'll be something different,' Mr S said. 'Just look at it as a cultural excursion and be prepared for the smoke and the noise.'

'Is that your idea of culture?' my mom asked. 'She's going to think that Japan is all Pachinko parlours and karaoke bars if she spends much more time with you.'

'No.' He shook his head.

'No what?' My mom looked at him.

'No karaoke.'

His voice was casually disdainful. My mom paused, then shook her head bemusedly, sighing. 'You had better get going.' She stood up and began gathering her things together. 'Call me when you finish up.'

As we drove along the Kamogawa, the river running through the centre of Kyoto, Mr S tried to explain the basics of the game to me.

'It's pretty simple. The only thing you have to worry about is the dial. It controls the balls as they come out – the further you turn it, the further they shoot out. You want them to come out towards the centre, so that they have a better chance of falling into the slot.'

'OK. Is that it?'

'That's all you need to worry about.'

'That it?'

'That's it.'

'What's the very best thing you can get?'

Mr S tapped his fingers on the wheel. 'Well – there's this thing they call the Three Golden Crabs.' He paused. His voice grew slowly enthusiastic. 'It's like a Pachinko myth. An immediate payout of ten carts. A deluge of balls. All you have to do is hold the dial and wait for the balls to collect. Put cynically, it's the hook – the one that lures them in, and keeps them coming back for more.' He stopped, then looked at me. 'But all you should worry about is getting the balls into the slot. OK?'

'Yeah.' I paused. 'It sounds kind of confusing.'

'Well, there's a lot of stuff going on, but it's pretty simple once you get started.'

'What happens if I have to go to the bathroom in the middle of it?'

'You can't.'

'What do you mean I can't?'

'You can't. Once you start playing, you have to continue. That's the point.'

'What kind of point is that?'

'Listen, Miss America, that's how it works, OK? Just go before you play. You'll be fine.'

We pulled up to a large building on the river's edge, just adjacent to Kyoto's famed Gion district, that dreamscape place of *geishas* and teahouses, of narrow paths and hidden entrances. Mr S parked the car on a patch of asphalt turf. I got out and stared up at the building. The whole front was covered with a hysterically colourful façade. A multitude of *manga* characters paraded over its plywood surface, an assorted jumble of dewy eyes and milky thighs, hysterical smiles and pearly white teeth, hastily sketched washboard stomachs, thick manes of purple hair, bikini babes and terminator guys, guns and space ships and heaving bosoms. Astride this senseless scene, neon characters spelling PA-CHI-N-KO blinked and purred. It wasn't immediately obvious what palm trees and space robots had to do with the game of Pachinko, and if there was anything pornographic in the pictured scenarios, then it seemed to me that it wasn't so much in the literality of breasts and long thighs and bullybag pouches, but in the sheer illegibility of the juxtaposition, sea crabs dancing alongside spacemen and mermaids and hot air balloons.

We entered through a more sedate back entrance. The walkway leading up to the entrance was cluttered with a dense tangle of bicycles and motorbikes. A man of indeterminate age, face leathery and creased from the sun, stared at us with gaping eyes, hands in pockets. He seemed at a loose end. A plump woman with a no-nonsense air about her adjusted her opaque sun visor as she prepared to straddle her bicycle. Overhead, an arched covering of red tarpaulin cast a strange glow of light on the faces of the customers leaving and arriving; below our feet, a faded red carpet made a half-hearted attempt to lend some élan to the proceedings. I looked back at the man with the leathery face; he was standing as before, hands jiggling in pockets and weight shifting from leg to leg uneasily.

We passed a small booth to the left of the entrance. A young couple smiled excitedly as they left the booth, counting over a thick handful of bills. Behind them, a middle-aged matron in a beige trouser suit sedately handed the booth operator a small ticket. She stared straight ahead as she waited to collect her money. There was a brisk air of professional implacability to her expressionless face. She took her money and swiftly placed the envelope inside her handbag before snapping it shut and walking away.

'That's where they collect their earnings.'

'But I thought you got prizes – stuffed animals and handbags and things like that.'

'They have them too. But they also give out cash equivalents – it's more useful that way.'

'When did they start doing that?'

'Oh, it's been that way for ages. It's better business, you see. When they started giving out cash winnings, a whole new market for Pachinko sprang up. Students, young couples, housewives. There's a whole population of people who pay their bills with their Pachinko winnings.'

'Isn't that bad?'

'Well, it depends on how you look at it. It's great for the Pachinko parlours. It's great for people who need a bit of extra cash now and then. But I suppose it's a bit depressing when you think about the people who are playing because they need money to pay their electricity bill.'

'Why don't they get jobs?'

Mr S laughed. 'There's something called a recession happening in this country. You know – this little thing that screws up the economy and makes everyone poor? It's been going on for – oh, I don't know, ten years now. Do you Americans not know about things like this?'

'Of course we know about things like—'

'Well then, you must have heard about the unemployment rates in Japan. Who on earth is going to hire a middle-aged housewife who's never worked a day in her life? Who's going to hire an elderly businessman whose last company went bankrupt? Even the students, who are young and educated –

there's a hundred people applying for a single job. No – the people you'll see here are people who need other ways of making ends meet. That's just how it is.' He gave a vigorous nod of the head, as though to close the conversation, and then strode ahead.

We passed through the sliding doors into the parlour, and immediately we were confronted by a raucous din, the sound of pop music and loudspeaker announcements. I had the sensation of pushing through a wall of sound, and my movements suddenly felt thick and swollen. Mr S leaned over and said something to me, but I couldn't make out his words. I waved a hand in front of my ear and shook my head. He nodded and gestured for me to follow him.

The narrow aisles were thronged with machines. The customers sat before these machines on low, backless vinyl stools. It was a strangely unmoving tableau, set against the hectic noise of the room. Eyes glazed over and glued to the screens, the players sat with their legs crossed, cigarette in one hand and dial in the other, immobile amidst that tremendous washing of music and noise.

We were indeed surrounded by the idle and the

unemployed. Nobody else could be whiling away the afternoon hours of a weekday in a Pachinko parlour. There were a few people in their twenties of middling affluence, students presumably, but for the most part the place was filled with middle-aged men and women, housewives and unemployed men on welfare, all of whom carried with them traces of depression and poor health.

They comprised the underbelly of Japanese society – the underclass that was rarely, if ever, discussed. This was the population for whom the bursting of the Bubble merely meant that things went from bad to worse; for whom the Japanese dream of hard work and reward was simply irreconcilable with their present existence. And while so much concern had been granted the middle-class families whose sudden wealth had disappeared with the equally sudden bursting of the Bubble, little notice had been given to this quiet underclass, whose prospects passed from a countable few to none at all.

Looking at them now, it seemed as though their faces had long ago hardened into expressions of grizzled discontent. In contrast to the youths, they were dressed in clothes whose shabbiness was apparent at first glance, discount-rack polyester shirts or trousers of faded cotton, thick-soled white sneakers. None of the brand names so prevalent elsewhere in Japanese society were visible here, and instead they were clothed in an anonymous vacancy.

We passed a woman in her late forties, dyed hair pulled into a frizzy ponytail set high on her head. She wore calf-length pink leggings, white socks and black sling-back high heels. The fluorescent light bathed her in an excruciatingly honest brightness; her eyes were hooded and weary, and her hairline crumbled into a messy bank of dried and flaking skin. She chain-smoked as she played, one elbow propped on her thigh and a nearby ashtray harbouring a growing collection of lipstick-stained cigarette ends. As we passed, she moved her hand to tap her ash into a plastic cup. Her eyes remained fixed on the machine as she returned the cigarette to her mouth. A vague motion of inhalation struggled across her chest. From between her lips, a wisp of smoke escaped and drifted across the machine's screen.

The man sitting beside her was surrounded by crates

of silver balls. He was playing with a dogged persistence, clinging hard to the thread of his fading luck. A drooping moustache of mixed black and grey flopped over his lip. Dressed in purple jogging bottoms and a white T-shirt, he wore a plastic watch loosely strapped around his left wrist. In the reflective surface of his eyes you could almost see his good luck dwindling away, and as I watched he looked up and caught my eye. Embarrassed, I looked away.

Pantomiming energetically, Mr S pointed in the direction of the toilets. I nodded. As I walked over I noticed a few people seated on the benches outside. They looked exhausted, and I wondered what they could be waiting for, and why they didn't leave. An elderly man with finely pocked skin emerged from the men's room. His complexion was ashen, but he walked briskly enough towards the concession stand and ordered a coffee. He tipped the plastic cup towards his mouth, hand trembling. As the coffee went down, his body seemed to brighten visibly from its tonic, and he even smiled. I pushed open the swinging door leading to the toilets.

It was quieter in here, the noise outside muffled and

insulated by wrappings of material, pipe and tile. I locked myself into one of the cubicles, hiked my skirt up and plonked down on the toilet seat. It was pleasantly pre-heated, and ranged along one side were the various buttons – sprays, temperature control, sound modulation – typical of a Japanese toilet. I sat for a few moments, lulled by the warmth of the seat and the relative quiet inside the cubicle. I swung my legs, hummed a tune, examined the tips of my hair for split ends.

The cubicle next to me whooshed enthusiastically, followed by the sound of a stall door opening and a firm clicking of heels. Suddenly self-conscious, I flushed and, pulling my underwear up and pressing my skirt down, followed suit.

A woman stood by the sinks. From the back and in the dim lighting of the place, she was only muted outline and shadow. She was wearing an inky blue suit, seamed stockings and black high heels. Her head, with its heavy arrangement of hair, drooped astride a long, pale neck. I could faintly make out the straightened seam of her stockings, the outline of her suit, nipped in at the waist and flaring subtly at the hips.

Her pitch-black hair was piled carefully on her head in the traditional Japanese arrangement, a rigid display of fanlike waves and knots. A discreet lacquer clip was pressed in at the bottom. Her pale face, shadowy in the mirror's reflection, was unexpectedly exquisite, otherworldly in the blurred fullness of the chin and cheeks, the deftly elongated eyes. Her eyebrows were thickly drawn in and the pout of her lips was carefully rouged; that makeup, densely powdered and inked, added to the spectral effect of her image in the glass. Heavily serene, she was like an apparition moving in the disjunction between the severity of her clothes and the ritual mass of her hair and face.

She was leaning forward towards the mirror and touching carefully at her hair with one hand. Leaning back again, she rinsed her hands with water. Moving with small, neatly controlled gestures, she opened her bag and drew out a delicate handkerchief. Drying her hands in a patting and dabbing motion, she looked into the mirror again before snapping her bag shut. Then, with a click of heels and a swing of doors, she was gone.

I waited a moment before approaching the sinks

and washing my own hands. I rinsed them hurriedly, avoiding the mirror, and then ducked out into the lobby.

Mr S was waiting. 'What took you so long?'

'Sorry.'

He shrugged and motioned for me to follow. I trailed after him as we weaved through the aisles in search of free machines.

'Hey,' I said, after a moment.

'What?' he shouted.

'*Hey.*'

'Yeah, hey, what?'

'I think I saw a *geisha* in the bathroom.'

'*What?*'

'*I think I saw a* geisha *in the bathroom!*'

'Oh, right.'

'Isn't that weird?'

'Not really. The Gion district is around the corner. I see them here a lot. I guess they're just taking a break before the evening shift.'

'Oh. Well, I thought it was kind of cool.'

'*What?*'

'*I thought it was cool.*'

'Cool? Why?'

'Well, you know, I've never seen one up close.'

'Christ – such a tourist.'

'Well, it *is* cool, isn't it?'

'*What?*'

'I said, it is cool, isn't it?'

'You know, it's a bit difficult to hold a conversation in all this racket.'

'Never mind.'

We continued moving along the aisles.

Mr S motioned me to sit down at a machine. 'This is a good one,' he shouted.

'How do you know?'

'What?'

'How do you know?' I shouted.

He shook his head. 'I'll explain later.' I sat down, and he inserted a five thousand yen bill into the machine. The machine sprang to life; on the computer inlaid across the centre of the machine, an *anime* character, blonde and buxom in bikini and flippers, swam across the screen.

'Turn the dial,' Mr S shouted.

I turned the dial. Immediately, a torrent of silver

balls bounced out from one side of the machine, ricocheting senselessly before dropping to the bottom of the machine. I turned to look at Mr S.

'No, no! They're going all over the place! You're turning the dial too far!'

I loosened my grip on the dial. With a gurgle, the spurt of balls disappeared.

He shook his head. 'Somewhere in the middle – try somewhere in the middle.'

I turned the dial midway, and in an even shower, the silver balls began to fall in what was evidently the right direction. Mr S nodded.

'Now what?' I shouted.

'Nothing. You just sit there and wait.'

'For what?'

'Just wait.' Mr S sat down at the machine next to me, and began to play. I stared at the screen. Nothing was happening. Bored, I tried twisting the dial full throttle. Immediately, the balls flew in a burst across the machine, before sinking impotent to the bottom.

'Don't do that!' shouted Mr S. 'You'll waste the balls.'

'This is boring!' I shouted back. He rolled his eyes at me exasperatedly. Resignedly, I directed the balls back towards the centre. Hand on dial, I twisted my neck to look around. The aisle was still with silent, crouching figures. A young man wearing yellow-tinted sunglasses entered the aisle, looking for a seat. He stared at me for a moment, puzzled. Then, gesturing to an assistant for a cup of coffee, he sat down and began playing. Overhead, music videos flashed across a television screen.

I turned my attention back to the machine. The screen had suddenly come to life. The buxom girl waved excitedly before swimming off, and was replaced by a slot machine mechanism. The icons – various sea creatures – spun round merrily, and as they met an approximate match – two crabs and one shark, three octopuses, two squid and one dolphin – a slow trickle of silver balls fell out of the machine.

'That's good!' Mr S shouted. I nodded.

A pile of balls accumulated reluctantly at the bottom of the machine. The icons continued spinning into minor matches and mismatches, according to which an unspecified tally of balls was yielded. The slot machine spun with awesome energy, pausing breathlessly over two-dolphin-one-goldfish, three-red-squid, two-crabs-one-swordfish, three-sharks, two-starfish-one-turtle, one-dolphin-one-whale-one-turtle, rattling out the tongue-twisting combinations with nary a gasp of uncertainty. Down below, the machine hiccupped and burped out silver balls with perfunctory regularity. And then, quite unexpectedly, the machine slowed to a delicious stop over a matched line of three gold crabs.

I looked up at Mr S. For a long moment the gold crabs sat there, one atop the other, winking and blinking knowingly at me. I stared back at them, open mouthed with surprise. Then, the crabs flew away and the buxom girl appeared, jumping up and down elatedly, breasts trembling and arms waving in the air. A row of lights burst into colour and ran frantically along the edge of the monitor. The machine, overcome with excitement, began rocking back and forth, howling out impatiently before coming to a restless halt. The buxom girl continued jumping about on the screen, eyes glistening sentimentally.

Mr S, and several other people, turned to look. His eyes widened; then, nodding enthusiastically, he slapped my back in congratulations.

'What just happened? What do I do now?' I shouted.

Mr S only nodded his head again and gave me a thumbs-up sign. From out of nowhere, a uniformed assistant appeared. He carried an exuberant sign, emblazoned with three golden crabs and an array of glitter-encrusted *kanji* characters I couldn't identify. He affixed the sign to my machine before peering at the screen and smiling friendly at me. I smiled back nervously, spine crouched and holding the dial with one hand ('all you have to do is hold the dial and wait for the balls to collect') in what I hoped appeared a practised stance.

As if coaxed into the madness of an extreme good humour, the machine was now loudly singing a tuneless ditty to itself. The buxom girl waved a final, ecstatic goodbye, and was replaced by the slot machine, on which the old icons of the sea were spinning round in a hysterical blur. Then, icons still spinning and without obvious reason or explanation, an inundation of silver balls erupted from the bottom of the machine. The clatter, as the balls fell into the cart, was deafening. It was as if the machine was racked by fits of acute indigestion and spewing out the sum total of its insides.

Within moments, the cart catching the balls was full. A different assistant appeared and exchanged the full cart for an empty one. He too smiled his congratulations. A third assistant set down a cup of coffee by the side of my machine, and offered me a hot towel. As the violent emissions continued to flush out from the bowels of the machine, I suddenly found myself the centre of immediate attention, congratulation and goodwill.

The full cart was parked behind my stool. A minute later, the new cart grew full, was duly exchanged for an empty one, and so on until there were eight full carts and counting, piled up around me like buccaneer's bounty. People were staring; a man seated several places down growled discontentedly before standing up and departing. I chortled gloatingly.

Next to me, Mr S was having less luck. Irritated, he lit a cigarette and recrossed his legs. The avalanche of silver balls continued without pause. He got up and shouted, 'Something to drink?' before disappearing. I continued to sit before the machine. Every few minutes, an assistant appeared to exchange the carts and generally exude helpfulness and congratulations. The complimentary coffee sat untouched, cooling.

As I continued to sit there, stomach aching with a

dizzy sense of gratification, I realized how much this game exaggerated the sensation of a big win. Each basket was worth only five thousand yen, a little under fifty dollars; the point about the massive pile of silver balls behind me was not the several hundred dollars they represented, but the feel of winning they imparted. And for a country caught in the grip of an extended depression, a country with high rates of unemployment and under-employment, that feeling of winning was addictive. It gave a sense of artificial exuberance and good luck, a promise that the universe was after all not without its points of benevolence – and it was in search of that feeling, as much as any pecuniary compensation, that the unemployed and the elderly, the housewives trapped in their homes, came to these Pachinko parlours.

Mr S returned with two plastic cups filled with a brown liquid. He set one down next to me. A quickly dissolving island of brown powder floated on top of a murky liquid.

'Chocolate drink,' he said. I nodded and stirred the liquid with a finger. It was impeccably room temperature.

'Hot chocolate or chocolate milk?' I asked.

He shrugged. 'Chocolate drink,' he repeated.

I drank it down. It was thick and cloyingly sweet, and I coughed as it went down. The woman next to me had four empty coffee cups strewn messily around her machine. 'People sit here for hours,' Mr S shouted. 'They need the caffeine to stay up, I guess.' On the screen overhead, a young man in a white suit and panama hat was dancing energetically. 'It gets kind of boring.'

An hour later we stood in a daze outside the parlour. The relative silence of the street rang loudly in our ears after the incessant noise inside. I was exhausted.

'Eighty thousand yen!' Mr S said. 'That's not bad at all!'

I nodded. I could see why people were addicted to Pachinko; with eighty thousand yen, a single person or a clever housewife would be able to manage the household expenses for a month.

'You OK?' Mr S asked.

'Yeah, I think so. Why?'

'You look kind of grey.'

'I feel a bit sick.'

'All that smoke, maybe.'

'I think it was the chocolate drink.'

'Or the chocolate drink. Let's get some real food in you.'

As we started to walk towards the car, I turned back my head for one last look. They were sitting there still, haunting the place with the dull resignation of ghosts in limbo. Set amidst that ocean of noise, they moved with elongated gestures, silent and wraithlike. And as we left the place, I suddenly realized that the real nature of my good luck was indistinguishable from the ease of my departure, and the unlikelihood of my return.

The train now slows to a stop at Nagoya, and suited businessmen quickly fill the few vacant seats in the carriage. One such man claims the seat directly in front of me; flipping his briefcase up onto the rack above his head, he sits down with a hollow thud. From behind, I catch a brief glimpse of his face in profile, eyes shadowed and mouth drawn in a half-frown of fatigue. His suit, though, is immaculately pressed. Abruptly, he reclines his seat to its maximum, crosses his legs and settles into a practised sleep, the top of his hair visible to my eye. With the train thus full, and the seatback suddenly so close, the leisurely tempo of the journey fades, and I feel unreasonably compressed.

That visit to the Pachinko parlour was several years ago. On my most recent visit to Japan – that endlessly hot, summertime visit earlier this year and now through recollection increasingly so close as to seem almost continuous with my present stay – I came upon the same ghosts, displaced and in a different setting, but unmistakable nonetheless. I had accompanied my mother to the Daiwa Securities Bank, a bank dedicated to helping shareholders manage their accounts and portfolios. The Japanese stock market was then improving; it was, in fact, at that moment the highest performing market in the world. But that, as my mom drily observed, was only because the stock prices had fallen so low there was nowhere to fall but up.

We had timed our morning errands in order to arrive at the bank in the late-morning lull, but when we arrived there was still a short queue of people waiting to be served. We were instructed by the white-gloved attendant to take a ticket and wait until our number was called. Ticket in hand – no. 987 – we edged our way across the lobby and found a couple of spaces along the banquette seats in the waiting area. My mom picked up a fashion magazine from a rack near by, several months out of date.

We sat down. My mom opened the magazine with a vigorous snapping of the wrist and began perusing its contents – tips on how to achieve high-fashion looks on low-fashion budgets, the best buys in cosmetics and skin care. I looked around me. A thin, dusty light veiled the lobby, streaming in through clouded side windows. Passing through that watery sun, the figures in the lobby appeared ghostly and unreal. They were leaning against the public computer consoles, peering at the screens and scribbling notes in pencil; they were sitting slumped across the banquette seats, staring up at monitors delivering realtime share prices. A few of them simply stood in the middle of the floor, hands dropped at their sides and mouths propped open in paralysis.

Wherever they were, whoever they were, they had the air of having settled in. Some of them carried newspapers, but they remained unopened. Others carried briefcases or file folders, but they too remained closed.

My mom looked up from the magazine she was reading. 'They spend the morning here.'

'Who?'

'Them.' She nodded towards the watching figures with her head. '*Them*.'

'What are they doing?'

'Watching share prices. I don't know.'

'Why can't they do it at home?'

'I don't know.'

'Are they retired?'

'*I don't know*.' She paused. 'I think so. I think . . .' She hesitated, and then spoke reluctantly. 'I think they like coming here. They must like coming here. I mean, they spend hours at a time here, watching and watching. It's like they're obsessed.'

'Obsessed with what?'

'With the stock market. Your great-auntie was like that. Always checking on her portfolio. We used to joke about it, until we found out she had made a fortune playing the market. You never would have guessed it, to look at her. She looked just like a little old lady, maybe a little bit senile. You know – wearing old clothes and not really looking after herself. Nobody would have guessed from looking at her that she was actually . . .' She hesitated.

'Loaded?'

'Well, that too, but more that she was looking out for herself, and doing a good job of it. People didn't take her seriously. She was old. A retired housewife. Retired people don't count for much, in any society.'

That explained their look of quiet outrage. These were men and women well past the age of retirement, in their sixties and seventies perhaps; it was retirement's rude displacement that gave them that air of wandering homelessness. When I looked closer, I thought I could see traces of old cunning in their eyes as they tracked the sprees and falls of the market. I leaned towards my mom.

'Maybe they're waiting to be served. Like us.'

My mom shook her head. 'No. They're just hanging around. I've seen them here before. They never seem to leave.'

'Even if they are retired, how can they just stick around all day? Don't they get bored?'

'You don't get bored when you're addicted.'

'It's not really like an addiction.'

'Maybe. But in any case, they do seem to spend a lot of time here, don't they?'

'Why are they so worried about money?'

She laughed. 'Who isn't, nowadays? Everybody in Japan is worried about money. It's just a state of being. You get used to it.'

'But isn't the whole point of retirement that you can finally relax and stop worrying about money?'

'It's meant to be, yes.' She looked around. 'I mean, look at these people. How old do you think they are? Late sixties, say seventy? They were probably the ones who were on top during the Bubble. They had a few years to get used to having a whole lot of money, and then, just as they went into retirement, they saw it all go crashing down. Maybe they were lucky and hoarded all their money in a savings account somewhere, but more likely they invested in the stock market. So, offhand, I'd say they've had about well over a decade to get used to worrying about money.'

Maybe all ghosts were worried ones. It was true that the anxiety in their faces had settled into their skin alongside the creases of age. They had money-worry wrinkles around their eyes, fiscal furrows across their foreheads. It was that nervousness and unease, more than any measurable pallor of skin or light, that made them seem so unsubstantial as they stood in the carpeted lobby, that converted them from flesh-and-bone human beings into spectral presences.

If they were indeed in their sixties and seventies, then they would have been the chief architects of the Bubble, the ones directing that wave of economic madness, and riding high on the crest of its momentum. And, they would have been on the brink of retirement when the Bubble burst in 1990. They would have spent the last few years of their career watching everything they had built come tumbling down with a crash, and they would have been ushered into retirement in the arms of uncertainty. If they had a habit of watching obsessively, then it was maybe not so surprising, because for a few brief years in the early Nineties, the stock markets, with their erratic fluctuations and their stunningly poor performances, seemed to hold the key not only to the security of their future, but to the enduring meaning of their past.

It was in the Eighties that the Japanese economy first surged to life as the most daunting of the Asian

Tigers, and during those years it seemed, as levels of productivity and rates of efficiency climbed ever higher, genuinely unstoppable. Everybody was rich. Everybody had money. I remember it as a child, watching from America. My cousins, aunts and uncles, the whole of my Japanese family, were suddenly flush with money. Their homes were bulging with material things – with the latest Nintendo game consoles that would not be available in America for another six months, with electronic remote-control cars, with plush leather sofas and endless racks of costly clothes, with Mercedes Benz station wagons and BMW convertibles. They ate out almost every night, and when they ordered delivery, it was not pizza, or Chinese food, but platters of the finest sushi and sashimi.

Simultaneously, my parents watched as the Japanese economy came bounding into the columns of American newspapers and magazines, business reports and television news stories. A dense accumulation of sensations – wonder and astonishment, fear and anxiety, greed and hope – gathered around the idea of the Japanese economy. Around the enchanting idea of its unfailing success – but also around the human character of that success. Because the real source of the tremendous noise around the Bubble, the human-interest angle to the fiscal story, was in the indomitable, selfless work ethic of the Japanese. In the way the economy seemed to climb, expanding to such vertiginous heights, on the labours of a nation that believed in hard work and sacrifice, and did not hesitate to direct the hoist and pull of their personal ambition into those channels sanctioned by society.

Technically speaking, the Bubble was nothing more than endless rows of numbers and figures, cold unfeeling units of data, but it was all somehow linked back to the idea of a nation, of a national character. What most fascinated and bewildered the Western world was the notion that the Japanese worker, the typical *salaryman* with his homemaker wife and two children, was working endlessly at the office in the name of a cause above and beyond personal advancement; that he lost count of overtime hours because he believed in the idea of building a nation. It was at about this time that the word *salaryman* became as common to the world as *kamikaze* had been in another time.

This was a notion of economic strength that was

deeply invested in the idea of national power – and, however intuitively, America seemed to understand both the threat and the allure of that nationalism. If there was a certain hysteria to the boycott of Japanese companies in the Eighties, to the sweeping imperative 'Buy American!', then that was because America understood that the surge in the Japanese economy related to an idea of power that was subconsciously linked to the path of a long recovery. A recovery from war scars and war shames, easily invoked in the sounding of single words, simple syllables: Hiroshima, Nagasaki, Okinawa.

'I think it was about then,' I remember my mom saying, 'that we finally got over the idea that white people were better than us. Up until then, for as long as I can remember, we thought that white people were better than us. It now seems crazy, unthinkable. But that is what occupation – not just military occupation, but cultural occupation, ideological and psychological occupation – does to a country. That is what total defeat does. We were so stupid. We believed it, for so long. But that's ended now.' The long process of recovery finally seemed complete when, during the

Eighties, Japan emerged as a plausible world power, in the face of which America itself was daunted. And perhaps for a brief moment, in the midst of boycotting Toyota, America dimly imagined that this surge in the Japanese economy was merely the second act to a more violent struggle enacted some fifty years earlier.

Our number was called, the digits 9–8–7 flashing in red across the little digital display. A mechanical female voice addressed us from the PA system.

'Customer 9–8–7. Thank you for waiting. Please go to desk four.'

With a sigh my mom replaced the magazine. Gathering our things, we walked up to the desk. A little teller with a coiffed bob, neatly middle-aged, blinked at us from behind the desk.

'May I see your ticket, please?'

Patiently, my mom slid the scrap of paper across to the teller. Using both hands, she picked it up, examined it closely, and then slid it to one side of the desk.

'May I apologize for the wait. How can I help you today?'

The teller was rosy cheeked, and she had the plumpness of a good piece of poultry. She held her eyes wide open and moved her head with quick, alert gestures, nodding and pursing her mouth as my mom spoke. While the teller was busy punching at her keyboard, my mom abruptly asked, 'How is Hankyu doing by the way?'

The little teller inclined her head. Her fingers slowed, then came to a halt. She wheeled round in her chair to face my mother. She took in a breath, then exhaled. 'It's gone up a bit.' She paused and tilted her head. 'Let me just get the figures for you.' She wheeled back to face her computer, fingers darting at the keyboard.

'Let's see. At the moment it's 405, it started the day at 395. It's been fluctuating around there, but going up steadily!' She spoke enthusiastically.

'That's good,' my mom said thoughtfully.

'Yes, very good. It's very good indeed – it's doing well!' the little teller said, ruffled feathers showing in her voice.

'Has it gone up a lot?' I asked my mom, as the little teller watched us.

'Well, yes. It was around 300 not long ago.' She raised her voice and, casting a sidelong glance at the teller, said, 'It really has gone up a lot!' Then she lowered her voice and spoke to me more confidentially. 'I think your grandmother bought the stock at around 1200. It's inherited stock, you see. She bought them right at the height of the Bubble. But for us – 400 is good. We'll take 400.' She shrugged.

The little teller looked at my mom and cleared her throat. 'Anything else?' She held her fingers poised over the keyboard expectantly.

My mom paused. 'Haltech?'

'Ah.' The little teller shook her head sadly. Her voice seemed to falter and then slow into reluctance. 'Not so good I'm afraid.'

'Yes,' my mom said. 'It seems to be in a steady decline.'

'Just a moment. The figures are coming up. Ah!' she cried in dismay. 'Not so good, not so good at all!'

'What is it?'

'180. Down twenty yen from 200.'

'Right. I suppose really we should just dump them and invest elsewhere,' she mused. 'They don't show any likelihood of picking up. I think things might be over for Haltech.'

The little teller looked both ways before leaning forward over the desk. 'They say that steel prices should go up,' she whispered confidentially.

'What's that?' my mom asked, absently.

The little teller shut her jaw with a firm click and leaned back from the desk. My mom looked up and stared at her. The little teller stared back.

'She said –' I began. The little teller's eyes darted to my face.

'At least I think she said –' I paused. The little teller's mouth grew more pinched. She stared at me, eyes bulging with meaning. I cleared my throat.

'I think she might have said, maybe, though I'm not sure, that there is a chance, possibly, that steel companies . . .' I trailed off. The little teller nodded her plump chin imperceptibly. '. . . are a good thing to have around?'

'What are you talking about?' my mom asked. She turned to look at me. She turned to look at the little teller. We both stared back at her. She sighed. 'Anyway, I don't suppose it matters all that much. Everything seems to be going down. I mean, granted they go up for a little bit,' she said with a wave of her hand

and a concessionary nod towards the teller. 'But the general long-term forecast is always facing downwards.' The little teller blinked her eyes sympathetically. My mom stood up. She snapped her handbag shut and gathered her papers.

'Well, thank you very much for your help.'

'Thank you for coming in,' the little teller said formally. She was standing, and bowed from behind the desk. 'Please have a pleasant day.'

As we walked out, my mom said in a low voice, 'What were you babbling about back there, about steel companies being a good thing to have *around*?'

'I was paraphrasing. The teller said something about steel companies being expected to go up, and then she went all funny and quiet.'

'Haltech *is* a steel company.'

'Maybe she was trying to say that you should hang on to it, then.'

'There's no way that was what she was trying to say. The stock goes down a bit more every day. The company doesn't diversify, it can't adjust. It's a lost cause.'

'Well, maybe she was saying you should invest in *other* steel companies.'

'How on earth would she know, anyway?' my mom asked, exasperated. 'Why is she the stock market guru all of a sudden?'

'She does watch the market all day. I mean, it's kind of her job. She must know at least as much as all those retired people hanging out in the lobby.'

'That's what you'd think. But the truth is, when things are going down, they just keep going down and no amount of knowing or watching the market is going to help. You can move your shares around as much as you like, but in the end it's pretty much all the same.'

'The same being what?'

'Being – well, bad to worse, bad to worse. The prognosis has been the same for the past fourteen years, and it's not going to change any time soon. The sad thing is that your grandmother paid a fortune for these shares – all of them. They're only worth a quarter of what she paid, maybe less. It's so sad, because she thought she was leaving behind a nice nest egg for her children, but things changed.'

Things changed. Because, of course, the Bubble burst. Did it in fact happen, as it seemed, overnight? One of the last nights that crowded in before the start of a new year, 1990, a new year and a new decade – was it possible that panic could be so efficient? That a national economy could so quickly flounder and then flop face down, beyond help or hope in an irreversible rigor mortis? Inflation, overvaluation, speculation, yes – but who would have guessed that the insubstantial world of numbers could wield such devastatingly real effect on the day-to-day life of a country?

In Tokyo, Osaka, all across Japan, an ominous still-ness settled in. People were filled with dread, because they knew that something very bad had happened, a catastrophe beyond their control, like a meteor flinging its way through the night. They were afraid. Afraid to spend money, afraid to be out shopping, eating in restaurants, driving their cars. Fearful for their jobs and fretting over their futures, they were too scared to move, and were trapped in the irrationality of a paralysis that had leapt its way into their lives over-night. They combed the newspapers, the financial reports. They reviewed their portfolios, the records of performance, trying to find the origins of a cataclysm they suddenly knew had been a long time coming.

And then, step by step, their fears ceased to be paranoid nightmares, and became instead the slow trickling delineation of their new reality. One by one, the feudally loyal *salarymen* were fired. They took to passing the day in coffee shops and in parks, newly idle after a lifetime of daunting activity. Sitting on public benches with empty briefcases resting on their knees, they became the emblem of a stagnant economy. The smaller companies, formerly run by intrepid entrepreneurs, shut down. The suicide rates went up. Abandoned building sites began to appear, projects hastily ditched as funding failed to come through. Those building sites of wasted steel and half-erected frames were only the more literal signs of an abandonment that was taking place on a larger scale all across the country, as share prices fell, businesses folded, and unemployment rates inched further up.

All this seemed to happen overnight. And within a year, maybe two years, people began to wonder whether the economy would ever pick up. A recession will never last longer than eighteen months, the sages and oracles said, bobbing their heads wisely. Give it eighteen months, max. Eighteen months passed. The sages and oracles adjusted their spectacles, cleared their throats. It was not so much a recession, they said, but a depression. Not to worry. Things would eventually look up. People looked at them despairingly. Blinking, the sages and oracles backpedalled. It might be a slow recovery – we never said recovery would be immediate – but recovery would come. It was only a matter of time. They flipped through their books, looking for new prophecies; they made things up. An economy with such a solid infrastructure, so outstanding a work force, was bound to come back up on top. Give it a few years, they said. And then they slammed their books shut and closed up shop.

Almost fifteen years later, the repercussions of the bursting of the Bubble – the audible pop heard all around the world – were still being played out. The worst had not come at once, crowded into those early years that ushered in the Nineties. No, the worst had spread itself thickly across the years leading up to the millennial celebrations around the world, the countdown in Times Square, the conspiracy theories regarding computer settings and the doubting hope of chaos, all the way up to the eve of that hectic carousel and then past it, trickling over indefinitely into the future. It continued for so long precisely because the Japanese infrastructure appeared so solid, and the work force so wonderfully motivated; because they clung tooth and nail to what they had, and disenchantment took a very long time to settle in.

Nothing, not even calamity, can move so quickly. But it was the bitterness of disproportion that made things seem so instantaneous, for if the aftermath of the Bubble unfurled for too many years, then the economy decimated by the Bubble was the product of too many decades. It was a slow build placed upon the foundation razed and then assembled again by the preceding generation – the generation that had lived before and through and then after the war. It was the case everywhere, on larger and smaller stages, in the national economy, in local family businesses. And it was for this reason that the devastated Bubble economy bore such a memorable, personal face of woe.

Such was, inevitably, the case with my mother's own family. The family business, which rode so high on the Bubble, was built out of post-war rubble by her father. My grandfather was the patriarchal legend in the family, the one nobody could live up to. His life story was one I had heard so many times that it was lodged somewhere between truth and myth, and ratified mostly by belief. (I never knew him, and have no memories of him; he died while I was too young to remember, a case of failed synchronicity, a source of regret.) Abandoned by his parents and raised by grandparents, my grandfather left school when he was thirteen to work at menial jobs. He continued in this way until the tumult of the Second World War swept into his life and millions of others' lives, engendering a ruthless social levelling. He survived, and then bounded out into the freshly razed world of nation rebuilding. In an astonishingly slim handful of years, he established a business of such notable success that it seemed to have moved past such ideas as expansion and security and well into the home straight of permanence. And it was fed on such certainty that my mom, her brother and her sister, were born into the world. They adored and were in awe of their father, and the only time he ever let them down was in dying.

He died when he was sixty, just a few years before the Bubble. And my uncle – my feckless, carefree uncle, who had grown up with racing cars and fast living and whom nobody could imagine as the head of the family – inherited the company. Once the funeral services had concluded and my grandfather been buried, the whole family gathered round my uncle and in a unanimous chorus told him what a wonderful opportunity he was being given. The chance to make a name for himself, handed to him on the proverbial silver platter. Nobody pointed out that he could never really make a name for himself, only build upon or undo the family one. And so at a premature age he was forced to crawl up onto the throne of the family and the business, and instructed to muddle through as best he could.

And he did. He managed everything – the company, the family assets, the family name itself – with surprising proficiency for well over a decade. My grandmother helped him, but everybody had to admit that they were surprised by his success, and that perhaps they had been wrong in their judgement of him. The company grew, and then grew, and then grew again, puffed up to astonishing heights. In those years – the years before we knew that this unnatural growth was the growth of a Bubble economy, and believed it was simply the signs of hard work and a growing market – we observed the material evidence of his success. An enormous house in the centre of Tokyo, the fast cars of his childhood resurrected and returned, widescreen televisions in every room of the house. He put on weight, his smile grew loose and generous, and at about the same time, his manner became more imperious, perhaps because he spent the day ordering people about.

But then the Bubble burst. The economy crashed, and then it grew worse, showing no signs of improvement. Everybody held their breath, waited for the phone call. But calamity worked at its leisure. It hid its face, bided its time. The company seemed to be doing OK. They didn't want to fire anybody – they didn't believe in it. They would get through this together, no problem. A couple of years passed, then five. It seemed as though they had cleared the woods, made it through the roughest patch. Some minor signs of economic resuscitation emerged, and, unanimously, everybody felt they had the right to exhale. They had made it.

But even as the economy began to show slow signs of recovery, things in the company were failing to improve. The figures should have been picking up, should have been righting themselves, but they weren't. My uncle puzzled over them every evening in private misery, half-disbelieving, even as the figures assured him that the apparent victory of their survival had faltered and given way to a mire of debts and creditors. Anxiety began to reproduce itself in a diseased pattern that, over time, overcame my uncle. Perhaps it was his fault – perhaps he had made strategic mistakes, perhaps he had grown lazy and complacent, or perhaps it was just that the company had been running on the steam of his father's success all those years. He didn't know. In truth, it was only the Bubble that had kept things afloat for so long, and his was just one of the thousands of companies in Japan whose dreams shattered and then fell to dust.

Just after the new millennium was rung in triumphantly and Japan entered its second decade of a seemingly permanent recession, the company went bankrupt. Calamity arrived at long last with its army of rented furies, and began tearing everything to pieces.

They went through the accounts, itemized the contents of the house, measured out liquidation with terrifying efficiency. After so long a deferral, it seemed hard to believe. But there were certain unshakeable truths that were beyond the shallow hopes of denial. The company was past salvaging or recovery, and as the news spread, the family name was gutted and left hollow, meaningless as an obsolete sign bent in two and resting on a scrap heap.

The family shook itself and declared its solidarity. The children said they would find work; the sisters said they would offer what money they could. Help was proffered from unexpected corners, and for a single, trembling moment it looked as though strength of family would overcome that of misfortune. But as the material facts of adversity declared themselves in more and more ways – in the foreclosure on the house that stood as proud testimony to the success of the family business, in the failure of the children to find employment, in the fatigue that showed itself, deeper and deeper, in my uncle's face, who finally took work as a delivery man, because *it was something*, and who was forced to swallow a feeling that was different from shame, that was not shame or humiliation but something else altogether – the family started to fall apart.

There were endless rows over the telephone, until it stopped ringing altogether, and silence spread in its place. Old jealousies were suddenly reasserted; old snubs and old wrongs were dredged up from the past and brooded over again. And those stories, flown out from Pandora's box, those aged arguments and tired animosities, once released, continued to swirl in the air, between the family, in the very rooms of the foreclosed house. Then, shortly thereafter and proving that misfortune cannot help but arrive in threes, my father was diagnosed with cancer and my grandmother with Alzheimer's, and then we could no longer worry about the company, or the foreclosed house, and the scrabbling of our minds went towards other causes for reparation.

In the end only such vapours remained, of all the bricks and mortar, steel and concrete, of all that currency and exchange, of the man-hours, the calculations, the boardroom meetings and the midnight telephone calls. Such was the legacy of those years, this long process of watching things slip away. Affluence, certainty and confidence, even health itself, all was carried away on the motion of a national crisis that was no different from an economic, and then a moral, illness. It was not how things were meant to be. It became, though, the way things turned out.

The furred smell of food filters through the air vents of the train, and then hunger comes upon me. A lazy hunger, bored and ever open to the suggestion of food advertisements spilling from the slow-turning pages of a magazine, the sight of a young woman, seated across the aisle and unwrapping a chicken cutlet sandwich. I watch her hungrily – the dainty movement of her fingers, the intimate rustling of cellophane pulling loose, the breaded edge of the cutlet, pressed between two thick slices of bread – then swallow and look away.

When, shortly before the end of the journey – the cutlet sandwich long eaten and the woman having stood up to dispose of the grease-stained wrapping – the food trolley comes round, manoeuvred down the aisle by a uniformed girl, pastel-coloured cap set on head and skirt pleated to the knees, I purchase a *bento* box, a can of hot green tea, and a box of chocolate-covered almonds. And as I eat, slowly, deliberately, the *bento* box balanced on my lap and the can, still warm, resting along the window's ledge, the familiarity of the food recollects the meals of my childhood in America. Those meals began in a time when my parents, more newly immigrated, clung steadfast to the food of their mother country, and extended through to the time when, the urging of American life and cooking having overcome us all, the influence of Japan was reduced to a simple side dish – a cucumber and seaweed salad dressed in vinegar, a plate of Japanese pickles – and then disappeared altogether.

And if returning to Japan can at times be so pleasurable, then that is because the food itself exists within a whirling mix of Western and Eastern influences, holding up at one end the purity of the traditional Japanese meal, and at the other a kind of lusty, degraded mix of flavours. And so, looking down at the meal that rests on my knees, moving my chopsticks from the fried chicken to the rice and pickles, methodically demolishing a soft-whipped mound of potato salad before setting down my chopsticks to shell the salted soy beans, I recollect those times in my childhood – the processes of recollection grown so inverted that, to recall my childhood in America, I am obliged to travel to present-day Japan – when the influences of Japan and America were equal, and there was no indication that that easy balance would ever grow loose and be forgotten, only to be tardily recollected so many years later.

But it is in a little temporal peculiarity, in a puzzling act of contortionism, that this meal, even as it flickers back into the past, also remains firmly entrenched in the telling of the present. And if as I eat, one part of me is shuttled back into the past, then I am simultaneously touched by matters closer at hand, reminded of the way that in our family, eating has of late grown altered again, and hunger become a new thing. Since my dad's operations (they cut out half his stomach, dismantled and removed his oesophagus, wrenched a portion of his colon upwards into their hollowed-out places, and then they closed him back up), we have watched as he has been forced to learn a new rhythm of ingestion, one that is parsimonious and slow. And we are always aware that he has not succeeded in teaching his hunger those same rules of moderation, so that his appetite is forever leaping out ahead of his newly stunted capacity to eat, discontented.

There are two kinds of empathy. One is a kind of mental acrobatics, in which the empathizer flies flipping and flopping and landing into the psychological state of the empathized. The other is less cunning, less deliberate, and occupies the body, so that the state of the empathized seeps stealthily into the body of the empathizer, catching him unawares. It is maybe out of the latter peculiar empathy that both my mom and I found ourselves feeding according to that same limping rhythm, whether in England or Japan: eating slowly, never eating enough, always hungry, but unable to eat faster, satiety achieving the quality of myth. And though there is the peculiar richness of associated memory in the eating of this meal, there is at the same time – in the slowness of my eating, in the absence of the compulsion that accompanies any true appetite – a reminder of the altered state of the present. There is a reminder of the reasons for my present journey, and the disjunction between times past and present is only thrown into sharper relief by the warmer comforts of nostalgic recognition.

A fellow bullet train whooshes past, bearing eastwards, the slogan *Ambitious Japan!* emblazoned across its shell. As its windows move by, with equal speed and in the opposite direction, the moment of its rollicking beside us as transient as the compounded speed of two trains moving on two separate courses, our own train is mirrored back upon us, the slogan *Ambitious Japan!*, with all its declaration of fading hopefulness, reading backwards and in ghostly characters. Once the train has passed I see, flying by in a jolt so fleeting it might have been imagined, a signpost for Kyushu. The sign is written both in English and Japanese, but it is the *kanji* characters spelling out 'Kyushu' that I read first. And though this seems impossible, the intricacies of *kanji* being long unknown to me, I am nonetheless left with a distinct feeling of prior acquaintance, turning round these particular characters, in this particular sequence.

Moments later I see another sign for Kyushu, characters whipping by with the same strange rapidity, and I realize the reason for its lucid familiarity is simple enough, explaining itself through the recollection of a near forgotten visit to Kyushu several years past. Embedded in that visit are pieces of the dislocation evoked by my meal, and then by the childhood it recalled, all of this linked together in the most tenuous, most fragile, of ways. And the thought occurs that it is just the spillage of associated memory that has coated everything round me with this feeling of possible recognition, drawing the flourish of association where none previously existed . . .

Though it was summertime, the day then, as now, was overcast. And the place was a strange one – a patch of land near Omura Bay, latticed with artificial canals, dotted with stunted windmills, covered in fields of vivid tulips, indifferent to season and perpetually fresh. People paced along empty streets paved with bricks imported from the Netherlands and built according to the precise science of Dutch engineering. They passed a fake version of Gouda Town Hall, they paused before an exact replica of the Domtoren. Ducks formed geometric Vs in the still water of the canal. Somewhere, a switch was thrown, and the windmills began to spin merrily, although the grey sky was still, and there was no wind.

This place was Huis ten Bosch, a theme park conceived during the Bubble years, and opened just after the fatal crash. The premise of the theme park – a painstaking recreation of a seventeenth-century Dutch town, a children's park devoted to Dutch architecture – was so ludicrous it could only have made the precarious leap from personal delusion to fully fledged and funded project during the mania of the Bubble years. As it was, the park's founder and visionary, one Yoshikuni Kamichika, had little difficulty in raising the required investment. Gripped in the green-lit delusion of creating 'a seaborn kingdom', he set to work building the park, pouring approximately 2.5 billion dollars into its miniature canals, extravagant replica buildings, manicured gardens and artificial windmills. Construction began in 1988, at the height of the Bubble. Two years later and halfway through the park's construction, the Bubble burst.

The park finally opened in 1992 and, from the start, was destined for failure. People were not travelling. People were not spending money. People were certainly not travelling hundreds of miles to a secluded bit of Kyushu to pay 4,800 yen to visit a hashed replica of an imaginary Dutch town. The inaugural year passed, and then the year after, and then the next. Those years that piled up one against the other were spent haemorrhaging money until the park had been bled dry and reduced to a pale version of its imagined self. The park's four hotels were perennially vacant. The boats on the canal ran sporadically, if at all, and the park began to gather the spectral dustiness of abandonment.

We visited the park during its tenth anniversary year. When we arrived, on that cloudy summer day, the park was deserted. There was no queue at the ticket booths, and when we paid and passed through the park's gates, we found ourselves standing in a plaza, neatly tended and empty apart from a lonely balloon man, standing in the crossroads holding up his colourful wares despairingly.

'Wow.' My dad whistled under his breath. 'Do you think there's anyone else in the park?'

'I don't like that balloon man,' my mom said nervously. 'I don't like the look of him.'

'He's selling balloons for God's sake. It's fine.'

'Then why are you whispering?'

'I'm not whispering.'

'You are.'

'Come on, you two,' I interrupted. 'Let's not just stand here.' I cleared my throat and opened up the park map that had been given me with my ticket. 'Look, we can ride the Canal Cruiser. It leaves from the dock over there.'

Avoiding the balloon man, we hurried over to the dock. My dad walked several paces ahead of us in a brave display of enthusiasm, and reached the dock first. He came to a stop in front of a sign and paused to read it.

'No good,' he called.

'Why?'

He shrugged. 'It only runs between two and four in the afternoon.' He craned his neck to look down at the map in my hands. 'Where's your mother?'

She was standing in front of a row of shops, edged along one side of the plaza. 'What time is it?' she called out.

'Eleven thirty.'

She peered in the windows. 'They should be open,' she said wonderingly. 'Look, it says ten to four, daily.' She rapped on a windowpane experimentally. The glass shivered, and then was still.

'Well.' My dad stood, hands on his hips. 'Well. Why don't we get something to eat? What kind of restaurants do they have here?'

'Dutch restaurants, I guess.' I shrugged and looked down at the map. '*De Rode Leeuw features an appetizing array of traditional Dutch cuisine,*' I read aloud. I paused. 'Or there's a Heineken brewery on the canal somewhere.'

'Surely it's a bit early?' my mom murmured.

'Or some rides, then,' my dad pursued.

'Are *any* of the shops open?' my mom asked.

'Can we just – focus?' I said exasperated.

'Why are you in such a bad mood?' My mom sniffed and opened her own map.

'I'm not in a bad mood, I'm just trying to come up with a game plan.'

'Have you seen anyone else? At all?' My mom looked at my dad. 'We can't possibly be the only people here.'

'There are people here,' I said. 'We're obviously

just in the wrong part of the park. OK. Look. There's a whole bunch of rides in this area.' I pointed to a section of the map. 'We'll go there.'

'OK,' my dad said. 'You're in charge.'

We walked along one of the canals. From dykes and windmills to brick and mortar houses, the reproductions were breathtakingly complete. The place, crowded with minute specification, was astonishing in its thoroughness. As we came upon replica after replica of buildings that we had seen countless times in their original incarnation, we could not help but thrill to the sense of a displaced recognition. Gradually, we found ourselves yielding to the hollow enchantment of the place. And in that succumbing we realized that, in a strange way, we had never really seen the original buildings; it was only at the precise moment of seeing them here, transplanted across thousands of miles, diminished in their proportion and their brand spanking newness but unmistakable nonetheless, it was only in that moment's strange and certain recognition that we saw those landmark constructions for the first time. In the end, you had to come all the way to Japan to find Holland.

'You know,' my dad said as we walked along. 'It's interesting, this place. I mean, you have to admit, it has its own kind of appeal.'

'I still haven't seen a single soul,' my mom said.

'Here,' I said, 'we're coming up to the replica of Gouda Town Hall.'

'There's a cheese factory inside the town hall.'

'What?' I looked at my mom. 'Why would there be a cheese factory inside a town hall? That doesn't make any sense.'

'Or a cheese festival or something.'

'Why?' I asked, baffled. A slow thought occurred to me. 'Oh, because it's *Gouda* Town Hall?'

My mom shrugged and sniffed again. The replica Gouda hall was adjacent to the replica Domtoren, the park's main attraction. A thin crowd of people had gathered at the base of the tower.

'Look. *People*. Finally.' I gestured in the direction of the fake Domtoren.

'Why would the Domtoren be in Gouda?' my dad asked wonderingly.

'What are they doing?' my mom asked.

'I don't know. It looks like they're waiting.' I looked

down at the map. 'I think you can go up the tower. Let's go.'

'I don't want to wait in line,' my mom said huffily.

My dad looked at her. 'We're in an amusement park. That's what you do in amusement parks. Stand in line all day.'

'But why should we stand in line when there are a dozen other attractions that have no wait at all?' She pointed in the other direction, down the canal. She was right. A few stray visitors were visible, but mostly that area of the park was deserted. It seemed as though the day's population of park visitors had concentrated themselves around the base of the Domtoren.

'OK,' my dad sighed resignedly. 'What's over there?'

'Astro Gebouw. Horizon Adventure. Crystal Dream,' my mom read from the map.

'Those sound *terrible*.'

'Come on, we have to give something a try. OK,' my dad said, squinting down at his map. 'Horizon Adventure. It's just around the corner.'

'What is it?'

'*Experience the power and destructive force of a flooding*

disaster in the Netherlands. Fog, lightning, waves, torrential rains and tornadoes created by the latest in high-tech flood and wave-making equipment combined with 800 tons of water make this an amazing experience.'

'Sounds pretty good. It says all that on the map?' I asked. My dad shrugged.

We headed towards Horizon Adventure, housed in a replica of an old Dutch East India Trading Company building. There was no queue, and smiling uniformed staff ushered us into a dimly lit auditorium. We sat down in uncomfortable theatre seats. There was an unconvincing stage-set, designed to look like a period Dutch street corner, and a lagoon of tranquil water that stretched from the stage to the audience.

'Do you think that's the 800 tons of water?' I whispered to my dad. He shrugged. 'Because it doesn't look like 800 tons of water. I mean, I don't know what 800 tons of water would look like, but I don't think it would look like that – you know, like a small to medium-sized swimming pool.' He ignored me and peered down at his map, adjusting his glasses.

A few other visitors trickled in. My dad looked at

his watch. The theatre doors swung shut, and the lights dimmed. The scant audience stirred itself expectantly. Lights pulled slowly across the stage floor and up onto the scenery, until a faux sunset effect was rendered on the cloth backdrop. A dulcet voice began speaking, disembodied and floating warmly over the audience.

'What are they saying?' I whispered.

'That there are a lot of floods in Holland,' my dad whispered back.

'Is that it?'

'And that the Dutch survived the floods due to their superior engineering.'

'What? I don't believe you. You're making that up.'

He tossed up his hands and shook his head. 'I'm not making it up.'

'You don't create an amusement park ride on the premise of Dutch engineering. Kids don't care about Dutch engineering.' On my other side, my mom had drifted off to sleep.

'Shh. The storm is starting,' my dad whispered reverentially.

A slow rain fell across the stage and onto the lagoon. 'That's not much of a storm,' I hissed. The rain picked up, and from over the speakers an energetic wind and thunder soundtrack began. The rain continued. A bolt of lightning shot across the stage. The rain continued. Ten minutes later, a pillar on the stage-set street corner fell to the ground with a loud, choreographed snap. The rain continued. I moved uncomfortably in my seat. The rain continued. Another ten minutes later and a current of half-hearted movement started up in the lagoon, much like the motion of a children's wave pool at a water park. The sprinklers above the stage gratuitously shot towards the audience for a moment, then returned to the stage and its steady downpour. The audience gasped in surprised displeasure.

'I'm wet, I'm wet,' my dad called.

'Do you think that was meant to happen?' I asked.

'What's going on?' my mom asked, woken from her sleep.

'Nothing,' my dad said. 'I think it's almost over.'

Even as he spoke, the clouds parted ways and the sprinklers slowed to a trickle, and then a halt. The faux sunset was back, shining on the backdrop. As we filed out, the fallen pillar miraculously returned to its original and upright position. The other visitors looked similarly wet and bemused as they dispersed down various paths.

'That wasn't so bad,' my mom said brightly.

'You slept through the whole thing,' my dad said.

'Well,' I said resignedly, 'we may as well try a few others.'

An hour later, we sat depressively in the Heineken beer garden, staring out over the canal. We had watched a fantastically kitsch animation video featuring overweight dancers and projected onto the 'screen' of a few vigorous fountains. We had sat in another theatre, this time unconvincingly made up as a Dutch ship, and watched a grainy video on Dutch history playing on a large cinema screen. At various points during the twenty-minute video, the 'ship' would let out a terrific groan and move unpersuasively in either direction. Half the attractions we visited bore signs reading 'Closed for repair' or 'Closed for remodelling' or, most convincingly, just 'Closed'. A late-afternoon shower settled in, dissuading all but the most determined of visitors to reboard the local train and head back to a saner civilization.

'I can't believe anybody invested money in this project in the first place,' I said as we sat drinking Coca-Cola in the beer garden. 'A theme park devoted to Dutch architecture could never have sounded like much of an investment opportunity.'

'Well, back in those days, they were throwing money at just about anything,' my mom said. 'There were loads of projects just like this one.'

'Loads?' I echoed. 'Just like this one?'

'Well, maybe not loads,' she conceded.

'I like this place,' my dad said suddenly. 'I like that it will never make money, or serve a discernible social purpose – that it's a billion-dollar pleasure park, completely without function.' As he stared across the canals, he paused. 'This park was somebody's dream, once upon a time. It was just a piece of imagination. And they turned that fantasy into real buildings, roads, real bridges and towers. They named it, they brought people here, they made it their own. And it's a beautiful place,' he said. 'No matter what you say. So much dreaming that went into it.'

Not long after our visit, we heard reports that the park was on the verge of bankruptcy. Its future perennially in question, the park continued its limping, half-hearted existence, bereft of visitors and waiting for the declaration of bankruptcy to descend. But it persisted all the same. And so the place languished there, like Kubla Khan's pleasure dome emptied of its dreams, the last vestiges of a time when anything was possible, and anything could be built.

The train pulls into Osaka, and with thoughts of that seaside colony's dubious persistence still in my mind, I am also reminded of the way that, however much health's certainty slipped into doubt, over the course of these years it also found its way towards recovery again – recovery being nothing like a restoration of the past, but rather the continuation of a present wrought through with alteration, touched by the unsteady rocking of constant and minute adjustment.

Outside the train, there is all around an architecture of persuasive staunchness, the stadiums and factories of Osaka slowly encroaching upon and then supplanting the fairytale landscape of Huis ten Bosch. The super expressways shuttle across a greying skyline, and the buildings are encased in scaffolding and dotted with cranes. In this landscape there is the assurance of continued productivity and the ticking of placid endurance, so that the process of memory becomes as plain as one foot placed before another, step following step all down the course of a vertiginous tightrope. And it occurs to me that the circumstances of the past, in retrospect seeming so secure, in truth was no different from these present conditions – the same tightrope, the same precipice across which it stretches, only then invisible. And if the tightrope, once seen, cannot be unseen again, then that is only the more stringent of memory's many conditions.

Now, as the train pulls into the station, destination achieved, I lean forward to peer through the window, knowing that I cannot expect to see them for several seconds more, hoping all the same that they will some-how appear early, and then, just as I catch sight of them – my mom looking anxiously at the arrivals board up above, my dad looking hard through the windows of the train, face rounder and with an extra sharpness to his eye, as if he held before him a picture of the world, newly brought into superadded focus – the train slows to an impossible slowness. And as I gaze out from the window they seem to hover just before me, approaching by the tempo of an exacting *lento*, measured out by an unseen maestro's baton.

15 August 1945, 11.59 a.m.

Somewhere on a swollen riverbank, an old man searches through atomic rubble. He walks, feet blistering, mind wandering, eyes misting over with dust and incomprehension. He stops a passing woman to ask for water. Barely pausing, she shakes her head and hurries on. At a deserted base, the last of the suicide pilots prepare to board their planes. Their gloved hands clutch at talismans of divided fortune: amulets of divinity, scraps of photographic paper. One of them adjusts the straps on his cap, then places his booted foot on the first rung of the ladder.

Somewhere outside the nation's fallen capital,

politicians and advisers stand in a makeshift war room. In two separate and lightless rooms, a mother serves her children a wartime dinner of rice and hot water, a cabinet member retires with a pistol and a migraine. Crouched inside the partial remnants of a burnt-out building, a radio technician fiddles with a toggle adjusting the rate of transmission, then nods the go-ahead.

A switch is thrown, and then the plastic wheels run rhythmic metres of dung-coloured tape through their spinning fingers. The sound ducks down wire and tubing, slipping through the narrowing arteries of the defeated nation. After the glitching of a brief pause, it emerges on the other side, spluttering onto the radio, and then the entire population of Japan is united in the motion of leaning closer – ears straining, backs bent. A long row of planes freezes to a stop on the runway, and stillness sweeps across the country in these, the last moments of the Emperor's divinity.

Then they hear the voice of a god that is no longer God, the voice of a god newly sunken in mortality – no longer divine, no longer sheathed in holy silence, but human instead. The voice is hesitant, and the people have to strain their disbelieving ears, so that these first sounds of fallen divinity grow blurred and confused in their heads, and their eyes drop tears for no reason at all. Then gradually, body piece by body piece, the flesh backed behind the ghostly voice comes into a slow and indelible focus they cannot shake away – first the tongue and throat, then the mouth moving in meaninglessness and the vague outline of a passionless face, the neck and body following close on, the pale slim hands and the surprising crudeness of the feet, flat and thick and clumsy – and then the myth of divinity, so long cherished, falls into slow and scrambled pieces.

In measured tones, the voice coldly relates the news of Japan's surrender. *We have ordered our government to communicate to the governments of the United States, Great Britain, China and the Soviet Union that our empire accepts the provisions of their joint declaration . . .*

An immense *whoosh* passes over the country, and then all is still again. In that stillness, the Emperor continues speaking.

We have resolved to pave the way for a grand peace for all the generations to come by enduring the unendurable and suffering what is insufferable . . .

175

In a historic radio announcement made on 15 August 1945, Hirohito broke the divine silence of the Emperor, and shattered the myth of the Emperor's immortality. In the last days of the war he paid the forfeit of his own divinity, moved by a tardy vision of enduring peace and the knowledge of irreparable mistakes. It was a fall further than defeat; a plummet whose distance was immeasurable, and velocity unknown. The record of where he landed remained a mystery, as did all the sights that must have passed before him on that fast downward arc through the cloud layer, passage singed by the smell of burning feathers. But he may have briefly fathomed, during the course of that long and silent fall, the heavy horizon of his slipped divinity; he may have seen, in a flash of hard insight, how his own fall would become entangled in an atomic aftermath so devastating it made mortality more fragile, and dislodged all myths.

THE ATOMIC AFTERMATH

Place: Hiroshima, Japan

'I'd like to welcome you to Family Day!'

Standing at the front of the room, she beamed, and in the enthusiasm of that beaming, her smile somehow grew stuck. As her gaze travelled across the assembled group, she groped at the ivory fabric gathered at her neck and cleared her throat noisily. They stared at her and waited.

She flashed them her paralysed smile again. 'I'm *very* happy to see the faces of so many family and friends – because to us, every one of you is *both* family and friend. As you know, we hold these Family Days once every three months, to allow family and residents the opportunity to gather together, here at Granda Homes.'

She was flanked on either side by uniformed staff. They stood listening, hands folded and heads pressed downwards. Dressed in pastel nurse uniforms and flat white shoes, they wore their hair neatly pinned up. As she stood there, one of them – a youngish girl with a softly wandering eye – slowly tucked back a stray lock of hair. Through the glazed doors leading to the kitchen, young girls in black waitress uniforms could be seen, plating dishes and arranging garnishes. A peaked chef's hat was briefly visible, bobbing in the foreground. A muffled voice cried out, 'Pork chops coming! Come on, come on, move it! Pork chops coming!'

The manager jerked her head towards the doors in a reflex of agitation. She cleared her throat for a second time. Her smile grew wider, showing the bright-flossed cleanness of her teeth. She began again. 'Family Day is an opportunity for families to get a sense of what daily life is like here. But it is also a cause for gathering and celebration.'

The children seated before her nodded politely;

the parents stared impassively. One of them leaned towards her daughter. 'What's she saying now?' she asked loudly. Turning their heads, the other children stared at the daughter.

'Shh, Mother. *Please*,' the daughter hushed. The mother snorted, then refolded her hands in her lap. The daughter smiled and continued to nod politely as she blushed. The manager observed them with a severe eye before continuing.

'And because today is a *special* day, the head chef of the Granda Care Homes Franchise is here to cook our lunch banquet.' The mother–daughter altercation appeared to have restored her buoyancy; she seemed visibly to hit a groove. Smiling, she clapped her hands together. Confused, a couple of children began applauding energetically. The parents maintained their blank stares. The manager nodded complacently, and then motioned for silence.

'Here at the Granda Care Homes, we have a rotating list of chefs, who weekly move from residence to residence. They each specialize in different cuisines, and with this programme of constant rotation we ensure that our meals *never* get dull. These highly trained chefs specialize in creating delicious, nutritious food for the residents, and work under the direction of our Head Chef, Asano Fumiko. Chef Asano is here today, cooking your lunch, and I believe –' she turned her head slightly – 'that he would like to say a few words to you.'

She stepped aside and looked towards the kitchen doors expectantly. The windowed doors remained still. A voice shouted out, 'Where's the white sauce? Where is it?' followed by a loud clattering of pans. 'Shit!' the voice cried.

Blinking, the manager leaned towards one of her staff, a young woman in a pastel-yellow overall. The young woman ducked through the swinging doors and disappeared into the kitchen. Several moments passed. Apprehensively, the manager glanced at the assembled families. The children looked back, wide-eyed. The parents were either dozing or muttering to themselves. The manager laughed, gesturing in the air meaninglessly, then swallowed hard.

A tall, bearded man in cook's whites appeared, hastily wiping his hands on his apron. He bowed apologetically to the manager, who looked at him askance, then turned to bow several times to the group, hands still caught up in the folds of his apron. The children gaped at him. The manager coughed, loudly. Sheepishly, he smoothed his apron down and began.

'I – well, let's see. I'm the Head Chef for the Granda chain.' Staring at the floor, he came to a long and unnatural pause, as if puzzled by the nature of the statement he had just made. The manager coughed. Reluctantly, he roused himself and continued.

'I oversee the menus and the production of meals for your parents – for the residents, I mean.' He looked nervously towards the manager. She stared straight ahead. He looked at the group. 'We've cooked a meal for you,' he added in a hopeful tone. He gazed back in the direction of the manager. Looking down, she carefully plucked an invisible hair from her sleeve.

He looked around despairingly. 'Thank you . . . very much?'

The manager broke into strident applause, nodding her head approvingly. Bowing awkwardly, the chef rushed back into the kitchen. The young woman in yellow reappeared. The manager stepped forward again, smiling broadly.

'I'd now like to invite you to enjoy your lunch. We'll ask you to step up to the buffet, table by table. Drinks are here –' gesturing to a table covered with pitchers of tea, water and juice. 'Please enjoy yourself. And if you need anything – *anything* at all – don't hesitate to ask me, or any one of my staff. We are here to help.'

Bowing, she stepped aside and motioned for her staff to gather. As she gave them vigorous instructions, gesturing towards tables and pointing emphatically, the swinging doors opened and the uniformed waitresses appeared, carrying platters and chafing dishes. A low murmur of stilted conversation ran round the room, and the children rose from their seats to fetch drinks for their parents.

'Well!' my grandmother said cheerily. She leaned conspiratorially towards the lady seated beside her. The lady was a very pretty old lady. Small as a child, she was dressed in girlish yellows and pinks and her hair was neatly curled. Her cheeks were rosy and, behind delicate gold spectacles, her eyes were bright and inquisitive. Beside her sat a middle-aged man with glasses and thinning hair; family resemblance marked him as her son.

'Well!' my grandmother said again. The tiny lady looked up at her.

'They give us nice food today,' the tiny lady commented. 'Not like usual.'

'Do they, now?' my grandmother said. She smiled cheerfully.

'Yes, they give us nice food today,' the tiny lady repeated. 'Not like usual – not like usual *at all*,' she repeated, giving her son a pointed look. Rolling his eyes, he tried and failed to suppress a sigh. He recrossed his legs, mouth set stoically.

'Well!' my grandmother said again. She looked at the tiny lady and laughed. Her eyes wandered over the room. 'So many people gathered here for the party,' she sighed happily. She smiled at me, and then at my mom. She turned to the tiny lady.

'Have I introduced you to my daughter and my granddaughter?' she asked.

'We've met already, Mother,' my mom said. The middle-aged man shot her a look of vague sympathy. The tiny lady nodded politely.

'Ah, and this is my son.' She gestured to the man beside her. He nodded, and my grandmother bowed, giggling. The tiny lady elbowed him ferociously. 'Say hello,' she hissed.

'Mother, you've introduced us three times already.'

'Nonsense,' she said fiercely. He shrugged.

'Nice to meet you,' my mom said, bowing from across the table.

'Nice to meet you, for the fourth time now.' He sighed, and then bowed.

'Look at Fujiwara-san,' the tiny lady said suddenly. She was peering across the room from over the top of her spectacles. 'She's far too old to be wearing that shade of red.' She jostled my grandmother by the arm. 'Look – look. Look at Fujiwara-san.' She picked up a fork and pointed across the room vigorously.

My grandmother gazed in the direction of the fork and clucked sympathetically. 'So many people gathered here! It's just like a party!'

'Did you hear me? I said, look at Fujiwara-san. Look at that red.' She shook her head, trembling with anger. 'She is far too old to be wearing that shade of red.'

'Mother, really,' the son said.

'What's that?' the tiny lady said. She cast a sharp glance at her son. 'Did you say something?'

'Just – calm down a bit, will you?'

'Calm down? *Calm down?* Do I look excited? Do I look like I need to calm down? I can barely move, how much more can I be expected to calm down?' Her son shrugged, and the tiny lady fell into a sullen silence, hand still clutching tightly at her fork.

My grandmother leaned towards my mom. 'See that table over there?' she whispered.

My mom turned to look at the table set diagonally opposite ours, where three geriatric widows were seated. Two of them were in wheelchairs; beside the chair of the third, an oversized walker was propped against the table. The frost-white hair on all three had thinned into stray patches, through which flaky, scalded scalp was visible. Exuding an extreme ill humour, they glared at the visitors and shouted obscenities at the residents they recognized. Their voices were surprisingly low and harsh. One of them pounded inanely at a bun with her spoon. Another slurped at her tea before spitting it out violently. A splash of dull-coloured grime flew across the table; it landed, shivering, on the cheek of the third widow. She looked up fiercely.

'They always sit at that table. They won't let

anybody else sit there.' My grandmother gasped slightly as she spoke. 'Even though there's always an extra space, nobody else is allowed to sit with them.' As we watched, the most decrepit of the trio shouted to a cluster of staff members, one of whom trotted over immediately. The widow beside her sat slumped in her wheelchair, glaring abstractedly at the wall. She growled in a low tone, and it occurred to me that she might be a man, stripped and denatured by age.

'I said, look at Fujiwara-san!' the tiny lady insisted. Exasperated, the son threw up his hands. The tiny lady pounded on the table with a fist. The glasses and cutlery leapt up brokenly. My mom looked alarmed, my grandmother turned towards the tiny lady and nodded sympathetically. Shaking his head, the son took off his glasses and rubbed his eyes. My mom gave him a look of polite commiseration. One of the uniformed staff looked in our direction, then hurried over.

'Can I help you get some drinks, perhaps?' she said. She massaged the tiny lady's back in small, soothing circles. 'Yamamoto-san, would you like some tea? Or juice?' She looked at my grandmother. 'Tea?'

'I'll get it,' I said. 'What would you like?'

'Just get a few glasses of juice and a few cups of tea,' my mom said wearily. I nodded and joined the queue at the drinks table. I returned a few minutes later carrying a tray with glasses of lurid orange juice and cups of hot tea.

'Yamamoto-san, some juice? Or tea?' my mom asked politely. The tiny lady glared at her suspiciously, and then, relenting, said, 'Some juice, please.' My mom placed a glass of juice before her, then looked questioningly towards the son.

'Tea, if you don't mind. That's very kind,' he said as my mom slid a cup of tea towards him.

'Mother – some tea, or juice?'

'Juice, please.' I handed my grandmother a glass. 'Thank you!' she said, carefully taking hold of the glass with both hands. She held it up in a toast, smiling, then sipped at the juice.

There was a glass of juice and a cup of tea left. 'Do you mind if I take the tea?' my mom asked.

'No, go ahead.'

My mom removed the juice and tea from the tray, and I stood up to return it. When I came back to the table, my mom was talking to the son.

'Well, unfortunately we don't live in the area. But still, I do try to come as often as I can.' She took a sip of tea.

'That's nice.'

'And you? Do you live near by?'

'Oh, yes, I do. But even so, it's difficult.' My mom nodded. 'My wife works too, and then our kids are preparing for college entrance examinations, so things are a bit hectic in our household.'

'I think we all do the best we can.' A pause fell, and she sipped at her tea again. My grandmother had drunk all her juice.

'Grandma, do you want more juice?' She looked up, smiling. 'Here, take mine. I'll go and get some more.'

'No, no, drink it. You're still growing.' She looked across the table at me, setting down her empty glass.

'So tell me.' She lowered her voice and leaned towards me. 'Have you found yourself a special somebody yet?'

I cleared my throat. 'Well, the thing is –'

I looked up. She had leaned back into her seat and was shaking her head sadly. 'Too much studying. Too many degrees. Nobody will want to marry you now.'

From across the table, my mom sighed. 'I wonder when it will be our turn to go up and get food.'

The son looked around. 'I think our table is next, actually.' As he spoke, a uniformed staff member came up to our table.

'If you'd like to help yourselves –' She gestured towards the buffet table. 'There are plates there.'

My grandmother and the tiny lady were deep in conversation. My mom looked towards them. She said hesitantly, 'I guess I'll just put a plate together for you, Mother?' My grandmother didn't respond. Snatches of their conversation, entirely asynchronous, floated up towards us.

'. . . but my son, who lives in Tokyo . . .'

'. . . I went only the other day and . . .'

'. . . it's very difficult, though, with the tele-phones . . .'

'. . . the pavement has turned grey . . .'

The son shook his head slightly and then stood up. The three of us walked to the buffet table.

Food lay prostrate across the table. Merely looking at it induced digestive exhaustion, and my stomach churned restlessly. Starting at one end with a diverse

array of cold appetizers (a radial tomato and moz-
zarella salad, braised endive with cream, a terrine
with sliced breads, foie gras with chestnuts, even slices
of pale pink salmon garnished with onion and capers),
it continued on in a regiment of portly black pots
holding soups and stews, shining double rows of
chafing dishes with hot pasta, braised meats, grilled
fish, steamed vegetables with sauce, potato gratin and
quiche. Mixed odours drifted on the steam that rose
above the table. At the tail end of the party were
appended plates of Chinese and Japanese noodles,
dumplings, sushi, some rice porridge. I reached for
a plate.

A stifled cooing drifted towards us. I paused, plate
in hand.

'What's that sound?'

'What sound?'

'That *sound*. It's like – pigeons or something.'

My mom turned her head. At a nearby table, an
elderly woman was quietly crying to herself. Long,
unminded tears coursed down her face, and the high
neck of her sweater was stained with a growing spot
of accumulated dampness. Her sobs drifted into a

low moaning, then into hiccupping sniffles. The other residents at the table were blithely chatting away as they ploughed through great mouthfuls of food, insensible to the sound of her crying. The elderly man seated next to the weeping lady peered at her untouched plate through bottle-thick glasses, then reached over and forked up a pork cutlet.

The sobbing grew into a more protracted bleating, and the woman's chest heaved expressively. One of the staff members turned her head. In a despairing gesture, the elderly lady covered her face with her hands and the sound withdrew, muffled.

My mom turned her attention back to the food. 'She cries all the time,' she explained calmly. 'She cries at every meal, she cries during the recreational activities, she cries during her daily walk. She can't stop.'

'Why?'

She shrugged.

We returned to the table, our plates laden with food. 'Here you go, Grandma,' I said, handing her a full plate.

She took the plate, and looked at it wonderingly. 'Where did this come from?'

'From the buffet.' She looked at me blankly. I pointed over my shoulder. 'You know – the buffet, over there?'

'Oh!' She looked down at the plate.

'Is it OK?' I asked, still standing. 'I can go back and get something else, if you like.'

'No, no, it looks delicious.'

The tiny lady chortled triumphantly. 'What did I tell you?' She looked up at us and nodded sagely. 'They give us nice food today. Not like the usual food.'

My grandmother nodded back and started eating. The food on her plate disappeared with prodigious rapidity. She ate without speaking, pausing only occasionally to wash the food down with long sips of orange drink. My mom watched, a small hardness setting in around her mouth. The food on her own plate remained untouched.

A waitress stopped at our table and took orders for tea and coffee; the manager followed close behind.

'Hello!' she said, swooping upon our table. 'I trust you found the lunch satisfactory? A modest spread, I know, but we do our best . . .'

My mom and the son made polite sounds of protest, which quickly died away into silence. The manager hovered over the table, her figure casting an obstreperous shadow.

Her eye fell upon my grandmother. 'Still eating?' She patted my grandmother's shoulder in a brisk display of professional affection. My grandmother paused, and lowered her chopsticks politely. The manager's hand lingered on her shoulder.

My grandmother turned to my mom. 'Who is she?' she whispered. 'Do I know her?'

Abruptly, the manager removed her hand from my grandmother's shoulder. The tiny lady snorted, and muttered something indistinct. The manager said hurriedly, 'If you'll excuse me, there are a few things I need to attend to –' My mom and the son nodded their thanks, and with a swish of grey suit the manager moved on to the next table.

'Beast,' the tiny lady muttered. '*Beast*.'

'Honestly, Mother,' the son said, teeth clenched. 'You get ruder by the minute.'

'I? Rude?' She looked at us in disbelief. 'So this is old age. My own son – *my very own son* – telling me I'm rude!' She pointed at him accusingly, then turned to us for support.

'We should be going,' my mom said hastily. She looked at my grandmother. 'Are you just about finished, Mother?'

My grandmother stood up slowly, leaning with her hands against the table.

'Here,' my mom said. 'We can take your dessert with you.' She reached over and picked up a plate of petits fours. 'Such a pleasure,' she murmured, bowing to the tiny lady and her son as she rose. Holding my grandmother by the elbow, she led her away from the table. As we headed towards the exit, my grandmother shuffling confusedly, we saw the manager start up towards us. Grimly, my mom quickened our pace.

We walked towards my grandmother's room. The care home was lavishly appointed throughout. Gilt mirrors hung from the walls and reflected nothing; plush carpeting ran underfoot, silencing the heaviest tread; in the sitting areas, mahogany armchairs were arranged in ghostly conversational positions. Everything looked new and unused, and although the place seemed empty, it was full to capacity. People appreciated that the Granda residences little resembled traditional care homes, though it was hard to know whether the luxury of the place was aimed at the comfort of its residents, or towards palliating the consciences of the children who had checked them in. The first week after she moved in, my grandmother called my mom every night to tell her she was staying in a hotel, but didn't know why.

'Wait, let me show you,' my grandmother said. She took me by the wrist and pulled me towards a balcony that backed off one of the sitting rooms. Tired, my mom sat down in an armchair and watched us.

My grandmother slid the glass door open and we stepped out.

'Beautiful, right?' She spoke in a tone of triumph.

The care home was tucked amidst the hills, high enough for the remainder of the town to recede into abstract, shadowy shapes. The hills were submerged in the lushness of a barely contained verdure, and a sea saltiness was tangible in the air.

'Do you see those apartment buildings over there?' My grandmother pointed towards a dark building not far off, spread low across the green of the hills. No lights seemed to be visible in the place, and its dark wooden walls were dank and rotting. I hadn't spotted it at first, so much did it ebb away into the dimness of the surrounding area.

I nodded.

'That used to be new,' she explained. 'But then they built newer apartments and everybody moved out of them.'

I waited, but there seemed to be no further point to her story. Sighing, she retreated back inside. I closed the sliding door behind us. My mom was watching us.

'Oof, I'm tired,' my grandmother said, suddenly.

'Let's go back to your room and have a rest,' my mom said, standing up. My grandmother nodded and began walking down the corridor. We followed close behind.

'What's that building over there?' I asked my mom in a whisper.

'What building?'

'That apartment building close by. It seems to bother her.'

'Oh yes.' My mom sighed. 'She's obsessed by that building. It's not an apartment building. It used to be a care home, like this one. I think it's gone out of business.'

'Oh.'

'I don't know how she found out. From one of the other residents, maybe.'

We arrived at my grandmother's room. 'Here we are,' she said. She sounded exhausted. She slid her shoes off and stepped into a pair of slippers before staggering forward towards her bed. She lay down, curled up on one side. She looked very small. 'I'm just going to have a little rest,' she said, eyes closing. 'Just a little tired,' she murmured.

I looked around the room. It was large, by Japanese standards. There was a corridor leading from the doorway into the main room; to the right of the corridor was a bathroom with safety-equipped toilet and bath; to the left a small kitchen with a sink and refrigerator. Inside the main room my grandmother's bed was pushed into one corner, and a low table rested in the centre. Several framed pictures of my grandfather hung on the wall, and a small altar rested on a lacquer cabinet.

My mom knelt down by the table.

'Do you want a cup of tea?' I asked. She nodded wearily.

When I returned from the kitchen, she was resting her chin in one hand and staring off into space. 'You OK?' I asked as I set the cup before her.

'I'm OK,' she said. 'Thanks.' She took a sip of tea.

I looked towards the bed. My grandmother was sleeping soundly, her breathing regular and even.

'Do you think she's getting worse?' I ventured to ask.

My mom paused before replying. 'Hard to tell. She seemed fine at lunch, I thought. But then she's good in social situations. She pulls herself together. I mean, you might even think, if you met her for the first time, that she just had a case of mild senility.'

'Right.'

'But still, she's deteriorating, bit by bit. She's started to not recognize people and, depending on how tired she is, she'll forget things that happened an hour ago, half an hour ago – ten minutes even. When she wakes up, for example, she won't remember the Family Day lunch, or even that she's eaten.'

She set the teacup down and sighed. 'But really,

I think it's all pretty standard. Right on schedule, you might say.' She gave a wry grimace, then fell silent.

On the bed, my grandmother was snoring, her breathing regular. Then she stirred very slightly, opening her eyes. She sat up slowly, dangling her legs over the end of the bed. She looked at us. Her eyes grew wide.

'You came to visit me!' Her voice was happy. 'When did you get here?' She struggled to rise from the bed, her stockinged feet flopping and fumbling for her slippers. 'I hope you weren't waiting long. What time is it? Are you hungry? We could go and get some lunch, what do you think?'

My mom turned towards her.

Of all plausible scenarios, this might perhaps be best – a repeat of past events, a composite drawn from former visits. In its very familiarity it will speak, however deceitfully, of a holding pattern, and we will be able to believe that after all not much has changed in the several months since our last visit over the summer.

If we find ourselves here longing for the inanity of repetition, it is because any departure from past events can only be negative. There is always the chance that this time she will not recognize us; that will have to happen one day, and then she will turn to me and, worse, to my mother, with the face she has spent these eighty years turning to strangers. There are many such possibilities that increasingly have to be countenanced, but also kept at bay with a long, hard arm, that they do not come rushing towards us precipitately and with too much determination. And so we are both, my mom and I, contemplating this perilous balance as we ride the bullet train bound for Hiroshima. We will spend several days there, visiting my grandmother, and then we will return to Osaka on New Year's Day, remaining there until I fly back to London.

It is a weekend, and the peak of holiday season at that, and so as the train burrows further west – for as it turns out, I am perpetually moving west, from Tokyo to Osaka and now to Hiroshima – its passengers mirror each other in negatives, one part solitary businessmen working overtime hours, one part families without their fathers. Across the aisle an elderly couple, grandmother and grandfather to the young woman and children travelling with them, sit facing towards me in a four-person seat.

The young mother is tired. There is brusqueness in her voice as she says a few brief words to the elderly woman, who nods, then leans over slowly to retrieve her bag, a fallen toy. From that abruptness, which speaks loudest in the young woman's voice, but then finds its echo in the lines gathering round her mouth and the tension in her eyebrows, my unstretched mind reaches for the lazy conclusion that she is their daughter. But as I look longer, eye sharpening, the lack of synchronicity (of gesture, of physical likeness, of philosophy and of affection) running loud between them indicates instead that the young woman has married into that abruptness.

Neither the blood familiarity of the in-law relationship nor its fracturing terseness is a surprise or rarity in this country, where it is common for three generations of life to grow up and old together. But that structure of ageing is growing strained. In 2003 the elderly population in Japan reached a record high.

There were more than 24 million people over 65 in Japan, accounting for 19 per cent of the population. It is currently predicted that by 2050, the aged population will account for over 35 per cent. The key working population – aged 25 to 50 – is dwindling; meanwhile, the population figures for the next generation are at an abysmal low. It is expected that the total Japanese population will peak in the year 2006, before entering a state of permanent decline. It is not clear to anyone exactly who will be doing the working, come the future, and it is not clear who will be caring for Japan's rapidly growing, rapidly ageing, population.

Japan has become a country for old people – a country of the retired, the prematurely senile, a country of aching joints. That country is evident even in a quick perusal of the train carriage. When I turn to look down the narrowed aisle running through the carriages, I see a collection of elderly men and women swaying to the motion of the train, their eyes bespectacled and their backs bent double. Outside, set above the blurring country landscape, a tower building darts towards the skyline: a work in progress, a newly built care home opening some time in the new year. Inside the carriage a large placard uses supersized font to advertise the national transport system's Silver Discount passes for senior citizens. This is, it seems, no country for young people.

Japan is ageing too fast. That is what all the reports, all the statistics, unanimously declare. That is what the constant worry over social security and medical care declares. They are not philosophical, the facts and figures; they do not believe in doubt or ambiguity, but dwell in absolutes. Japan is ageing faster than any other country in the world. All the speed that is stored within the Japanese system, all the hurrying and all the great efficiency, has had its most stringent effect on the population itself.

This is a country for the aged – and yet there is no place for the elderly in the society's chosen self-image. They have slowly been discounted. And though they know the toll of a century's worth of wars and depressions, though they hold a collective experience indistinguishable from the idea of the nation's legacy – despite all this, as disease and senility creep into the memory receptors of their brains, the ability to remember is crumbling to pieces. The retrieval mechanism breaks down, the filing system collapses, and they cannot retrieve the truth of their past lives.

When my grandmother was diagnosed with Stage II Alzheimer's (the precision of the diagnosis so unambiguous, and so irreversible), memory finally lost its fixity to me. Until then, I had thought of memory as something that subsisted in the banks of permanence; I had thought, even, that permanence was itself the purpose of memory. But as I witnessed the black holes that daily gnawed away at my grandmother's ability to remember, memory became mortal. Beyond its mere vagaries, its routine unreliability and its habits of lying, I suddenly recognized memory as something that would, with time, pass away.

And increasingly, the question that presents itself is this: what does she remember? My grandmother's memory is a mystery to me. There seems to be no rhyme or reason for what she remembers, and what she will forget; there is no consistency that can be traced or clung to. Even among the many brutalities of this disease, the failure of memory and recollection seems the cruellest. I do not know if she knows that she is forgetting, I do not know if she knows the truth of what is happening to her in that forgetting, and I cannot fathom how she makes sense of a world that is, increasingly, painted out with black gaps. Nor can I imagine the fate of these memories, lately grown extinct, the shape they take and the place to which they vanish.

And as I now consider and count those memories not yet claimed from her, memories of war, of country, of past and present – the memories of fleeing Korea with her parents, an ethnic Japanese born in the wrong country and under the wrong national conscience; the memories of her brother the *kamikaze* pilot, whose final mission chimed in time with the calamitous news of Japan's surrender (his plane was grounded at the last possible moment, and in that halting he found himself, having resolved upon a heroic death, the victim of a historical salvation fallen upon him from on high) – as I number those things that mark her generation from my mother's, and then from my own, the very personal nature of her disease subtly shifts, until it finds itself roving alongside, keeping loose company with, the parallel passage of history.

And it is in this way that I find myself now stumbling

over, now circling round, the question of how a country remembers, wondering what the collective memory of a country can resemble when every day another memory falls to pieces, unreclaimed and unobserved; what its mottled shades and its peculiar textures, what its capacity for longing, its thirst for retribution or forgiveness. And as I sit in silence on this westbound train, I wonder also what claims I can have to the reading of that memory, when so many of my own memories of Japan are themselves forgotten (lost memories of the many days and weeks and months spent here as a child; memories of a childish fluency in the Japanese tongue that faded as quickly as that extinguished facility; misplaced knowledge of my grandmother and my grandfather now dead), bartered for the continuity of my American childhood, for that longing to fit in that is so strong among children, and then so senseless in retrospect.

The loss of those memories strikes me harder now, during this present visit, perhaps because I am forced to recognize that what passes between my grandmother and me has, in a sense, become past history, beyond editing or recuperation. (And here I recall the number of times my grandmother, on the telephone or at the end of a too brief visit, gently entreated me to improve upon my Japanese, knowing then what I am only beginning to realize now, that I was not seeing her as she wished me to see her and, conversely, that she could not be seeing me the way I would wish her to see me, and that time's allocation was running short.) Nor can I, banked between my grandmother's present condition and my father's past cancer, ignore the fact that Japan is the country where my own parents will grow old. And so if those memories are important, then that is because it is through them that I will one day understand in what language and in what tones, in what tenor of voice, this place spoke to my parents, what claim it lay upon them that it so strongly drew them back to what they would, finally and irretrievably, call home.

The young woman with the children has dis-appeared to the dining car in search of food. The elderly couple attempt to engage the children. The boy is preoccupied with a portable gameplayer, and is impervious to their attempts to charm. When they ply him with bubble gum, with cookies and sweets, he whines, moving his head in an irritated motion before returning his attention to his game.

The younger girl is more willing. She accepts the bubble gum, the chocolates, with an eager, sticky palm. The grandfather roots about inside a rucksack, then pulls out a colourful plastic toy. Eyes brightening, the young girl reaches out to seize it. She wraps her fingers round the neck of the toy; the grandparents smile happily, and something in their smile reminds me of my dad, perhaps because the quality of the smile that we give to our kin is universal. Slowly, the haziness of the invocation grows more specific, until it locates itself inside the specificity of a singular recollection. A recent memory, only two weeks old, couched within the context of this present journey; but like all memories, it contains within it pockets of earlier times.

A group of scientists were huddled together in what appeared to be an enormous sandpit. Villagers in rough kimonos and sandals gathered around the edge and peered anxiously at the men. One of the scientists kneeled and cautiously plunged an instrument into the loosened soil in the pit. The apparatus emitted a short wail of warning; the arrow on the instrument's dial spun round violently.

The scientist stood up abruptly. 'This soil is contaminated!' he declared. He turned to the villagers. 'Get back!' he barked. 'Get back! This soil is contaminated!' They stared at him blankly and huddled closer together.

The head of the research group, an elderly man with greying hair and moustache and a weary air of pre-eminence, stared at the ground moodily. An entourage of younger scientists stood by and watched him respectfully. He moved several paces. He stopped, hands in pockets. He looked around him at the sandpit. A long moment passed before he declared, 'This is the footprint of a living creature!' The scientists around him gasped; in terror, the villagers wheeled away from the edge of the footprint and disappeared into the bushes.

The elderly pre-eminent scientist continued to move within the footprint, then kneeled down to retrieve a fossilized fragment from the soil. 'Sir, don't touch that!' warned the scientist with the instrument. 'That's contaminated! This soil is contaminated!' he repeated with conviction. The elderly scientist nodded, then leaned towards his young and attractive daughter, a member of the research team. 'This is a fossil from millions of years ago. How could it have ended up here?' They looked at each other. The mutual thought ran through their heads: what kind of creature left radioactive footprints and million-year-old fossils casually strewn in its wake?

A bell rang out across the island. The villagers looked up sharply, then began running towards elevated land. They appeared, armed with rifles and sticks, clutching at children and moving hastily along winding paths. The scientists watched them for a moment, then abandoned the sunken footprint and followed suit.

A distinct *boom* was heard. The villagers halted mid-stride.

Another *boom*.

The earth trembled. An animal scream erupted, somewhere in the distance.

The scientists came to a staggering stop beside the villagers. Their mouths gaped, and their faces were frozen in horror.

Slowly, the head of Godzilla appeared over a grassy hill. He peered cross-eyed at the villagers. They ran screaming down the slope.

'God, I love this movie!' my dad exclaimed, clapping his hands. 'Don't you just love it?'

If ever there was a mascot for Japan, if ever there was a character that occupied the collective imagination of a culture and a country, then it was Godzilla. Little children had been cheering Godzilla on since his debut in the 1954 film classic, which went on to spur over a dozen sequels, millions of Godzilla T-shirts, stuffed animals, action toys, plastic watches, bedding, patterned rice bowls, chopsticks, toothbrushes and, in 1998, a swish Hollywood makeover. In the twentieth century America had Mickey Mouse, a talking rodent with big ears and a squeaky voice; Japan had a radioactive, 400-foot, fire-breathing, ambiguously amphibious monster with little or no acting skills. But it didn't matter. Japanese children adored Godzilla (or *gojira*, according to the more Japanese pronunciation) in the same way chubby-cheeked, all-American children loved Mickey Mouse.

On our newly purchased wide-screen television –

an early Christmas gift to ourselves – two star-crossed lovers held each other in amorous panic. The elderly scientist was standing to one side, holding his hat in both hands and staring into space. The villagers bounced in and out of the frame, running and screaming energetically. From behind the grassy knoll Godzilla approached a bit closer, so that his truncated arms, as well as his head, were visible. He howled in abstract anguish, revealing multiple rows of sharp-looking teeth. Then, he turned and disappeared in a storm of renewed booming.

'Don't you love this movie?' my dad demanded. He was getting repetitive in his enthusiasm. He leaned over to pick up his tea; in the agitation of his delight, he spilled some over the cup's edge. It trickled down between his fingers. 'Shoot!' he said, reaching for a napkin. Wiping the cup, he leaned over and jogged my knee with one hand. 'Aren't you excited?'

My dad was a first-generation Godzilla fan. When the original film was released, he clocked in at an impressionable age five; it was in all respects a fateful encounter. Godzilla stalked his way through the mind's-eye of my dad's childhood, leaving a lifelong imprint from which his imagination never quite recovered. He continued, even as an adult, to harbour considerable interest in the giant monster. He faithfully supported the Godzilla industry by purchasing Godzilla models, mementoes, souvenir books and videotapes; he loyally watched the scurrilous sequels. But his favourite Godzilla film remained the original movie – The One That Started It All, as he liked to call it. And so when the new de luxe television/VHS player/DVD player arrived, it was natural that *Godzilla*, analogue special effects and all, should be called upon for the road test.

The scientists peered over the edge of a cliff. The camera panned to reveal a pattern of enormous footprints. They lined the beach in a loose S-shape, dragging back into the sea. My dad gazed dozily at the television screen, eyes enraptured. The camera cut to reveal a crowded boardroom. Journalists were pressed round its edges, scrawling notes and snapping photographs; a gaggle of panicked civilians attempted to force its way in, before being pushed out by security guards. Calm amidst this deft montage of chaos, the elderly scientist rose and approached the podium at the front of the room.

'Ah,' my dad said, nodding his head sagely. He leaned forward expectantly.

The old man looked out at the crowd, over which a hushed silence had fallen. Speaking in mild tones, he explained the team's findings before expounding upon his own conjectures regarding the origins of Godzilla. Using a nifty projector screen and terms like 'Jurassic Age' and 'Intermediary Species', he described Godzilla as a 400-foot Tyrannosaurus Rex with swimming capabilities (physiologically speaking, this seemed improbable, considering Godzilla's landlubber's thighs and decidedly non-amphibious physique, but nobody seemed to offer protest). He paused.

An image of Godzilla appeared on the projector screen. He was peeking out from behind a hill, and wore an expression of improbable coyness. His eyes had uncrossed themselves for the photograph, and on the whole, he was surprisingly photogenic. The assembled crowd murmured appreciatively.

'The question is,' the elderly scientist said solemnly,

'how does this animal reappear after so many centuries, and so close to the coast of Japan?' An animated hum ran through the room, and several frantic journalists waved their hands in the air.

My dad tilted his head to one side as he considered the picture of Godzilla. From out of the projector screen, a frozen Godzilla peered back, chin drawn down demurely. His truncated arms were modestly crossed over the edge of the slope, in the style favoured by shopping mall photography studios (a blue-sponged backdrop, a small, squirming child with pigtails, a teddy bear prop – Fabulous Fotos, Instant Images). My dad scratched his head, puzzled.

He looked at me plaintively. 'He never looks like that in the movie. How did they get that picture?'

'I don't know – a good press photographer?'

'Humph.' He looked at me reproachfully, then returned his attention to the television.

'It is my belief,' the scientist continued, 'that Godzilla was resurrected due to the repeated experiments of H-bombs.' The journalists scrawled furiously in their notebooks. A civilian bystander shrieked in dismay, and then collapsed. The scientist stared straight ahead, eyes bleak and mouth set.

In the swish Hollywood remake, the resurrected monster attacked New York rather than Tokyo – a shameless, if rather ironic, piece of revision. The original *Godzilla* was steeped in its own more relevant historicity; it was a film about the Second World War and the dropping of the nuclear bomb, about Hiroshima and Nagasaki as much as it was about monsters and inconveniently resurrected dinosaurs. Godzilla himself was always secondary to the havoc he caused, and the central character in the film was not, perhaps, the 400-foot monster, but rather the burnt and hollowed city of Tokyo.

The Japanese were never exactly vociferous about the fact that they were the only nation on earth qualified to attest to the real-life devastation of nuclear warfare. The film therefore contained only the barest sprinkling of a universally relevant cautionary wisdom (with the scientists strenuously repeating that they were 'afraid not just for Japan, but for the whole world'); for the most part these examples of moral advocacy were firmly tamped down, appearing only occasionally in what seemed to be uncalculated and irrepressible spurts. But it was a certain kind of cultural environment that produced a leviathan inexplicably wakened by H-bomb testing. It was one of the century's strangest ironies that, the world over, Godzilla was more instantly recognizable than the memorial cenotaph at Hiroshima. But perhaps this was always the point. In Godzilla the filmmakers had created a legend that would endure the most arid of cultural imaginations.

'What a great movie,' my dad murmured.

'I propose,' the elderly scientist said, 'that we send a group to do further research, but the main—'

'Ha!' my dad exclaimed. 'That is so Japanese! They're always forming research groups!'

'But he's saying—'

'National disaster, and they're organizing research groups!'

'—something else . . .'

'Japan will never progress so long as it continues to organize research groups!'

'Dad, wait.' Long pause. 'I think you've got it wrong. He just said they're going to use underwater missiles to get him.'

'Oh boy.' My dad took a deep breath, then exhaled noisily. *'Now he gets angry.'*

'What?'

'Shh. Watch.'

Godzilla didn't have a particularly wide emotional range; in fact, the only emotion he did seem to possess was rage. Godzilla stomping across the city, knocking down buildings; Godzilla chewing on a lamppost; Godzilla knocking over a bridge; Godzilla tilting his head back and opening his jaws in a rage-filled scream. Godzilla spent much of the movie angry. It was impossible to know quite what he was so angry about (apart, of course, from the numerous underwater missiles and military hardware that bombarded him throughout the course of the movie). His anger was more abstracted. It was all emotion. But we anticipated his rage. We couldn't wait for him to get angry, because it was his anger that set off the action of the film.

Scene: the streets of Tokyo, hours after the deployment of the underwater missiles. Victory was assumed. Crowds ran cheering, brandishing flags. A couple embraced enthusiastically. Children streamed through the street, waving their arms excitedly. Men toasted each other, laughing.

'God, it's just like V-Day, isn't it?'

'Yeah,' my dad said absently.

'It's like the V-Day Japan never had.'

'Shh.'

A cruiser boat, lined with lanterns, floated in Tokyo Harbour. The fair lights of Tokyo twinkled in the distance, but the painted backdrop of murky sunset was ominously still. On the main deck of the cruiser, young couples danced and swirled to celebratory music. A young girl, wearing her escort's suit jacket, leaned against the railings of the boat. Her boyfriend moved close to lean a cheek against her hair. An older woman in a low-cut dress laughed drunkenly. Two men crowded up against her and she tossed her head back, revealing the long length of her throat. A young woman shuffled by, dancing with her mother.

Mixed in among the gay music came a distant *Boom*.

'Here we go.'

The crowd continued to laugh and dance. *Boom*. The musicians faltered, and the scene fell silent. The crowd stopped its dancing and turned dread-filled faces towards the open sea. Godzilla emerged from the water, mouth open and roaring.

'He's covered in slime!'

'Radioactive slime –'

'Or is that just water? I can't tell with this black and white picture.'

'See, I told you he'd be pissed off.'

Pushing through the water of Tokyo Harbour, Godzilla emerged to his full height. He wore the expression of a sleeper prematurely roused from post-prandial slumber and grumpy with indigestion. Movements jerky and leaden, an outraged scowl fixed upon his face, he boomed his way towards Tokyo. He moved with grim inelegance, like an overweight matron emerging from a public wading pool; he held his weight with supreme awkwardness, waving his little arms ineffectually for balance.

'Why does he move like that?' I asked. 'It's like he got confused and thinks he's in a George Romero zombie movie.'

'He's supposed to move like that,' my dad said in hurt tones.

'Why is he "supposed" to move like that?'

'*Because.*'

'Because what?'

My dad sighed loudly. He paused for a moment, then waved the remote control at the TV with an air of resignation. The screen froze; Godzilla paused mid-roar, water droplet hanging from nostril. My dad turned to face me and adjusted his glasses professorially.

'Now, there are many things we love about the original *Godzilla*. The antique special effects. The clunky dialogue. But what we—'

'Who's we?'

'—appreciate most of all is this: possibly the greatest uncredited performance in movie history. People forget about the man who plays Godzilla; they forget the man in the Godzilla costume, stomping around a miniature set of Tokyo and knocking everything down. And yet, you see, he plays the role very carefully, accommodates the necessary binaries of the film. When you watch his performance, you see Godzilla, but you also see the man in the Godzilla suit. Now, that human aspect is central to the emotional integrity of the film. The man in the Godzilla suit allows the human aspect of the monster to come through, while simultaneously maintaining the fictional apparatus of the film. It's an example fully meriting the use of what is generally an overextended term: the bravura performance.' He paused. 'Right. Now observe, and try to appreciate.'

Picking up the remote control, he turned back to face the screen. Godzilla jolted into action, snarling. The water droplet flew off into oblivion.

I had a sudden image of my father as a child, tramping through the house in shorts and T-shirt. He emitted a roar and pounced on his mother at the kitchen stove. She let out a faint scream, a pan of peas tumbled to the floor. Catching her breath, she ordered him to clear up the peas and retire to his bedroom until dinnertime. Sulking, he kneeled on the floor and pretended he was Godzilla, picking off individual, pea-shaped civilians.

Godzilla appeared against a backdrop of telephone wires. As he roared, people ran screaming down the streets. A train shot by. He placed a scaly foot in the path of the train; the conductor winced in consternation; with a horrible screech, it crumpled like an accordion. Arms flailing, Godzilla bent over. When he straightened up, he had a train carriage clenched between his teeth. He chewed on it discontentedly for several seconds before spitting it out in disgust. He knocked over a few more bridges and batted at a few more telephone wires before disappearing into the harbour. The scientists watched thoughtfully.

The city was hastily evacuated. In a last-ditch effort to protect Tokyo, the military erected a 300,000-volt barrier around the city. Nightfall arrived. Brief but haunting shots of empty, evacuated streets. We were told that Tokyo was on 'watch and wait' status. Searchlights fanned across the water of Tokyo Harbour as Godzilla emerged again, splashing at the water with his arms. He lumbered awkwardly towards the shore. We got another good look at his costume, at the Godzilla suit.

'See, look at that,' my dad said. 'You can practically see the *fabric* they used to make the costume.' Thickly padded and shapeless, Godzilla was an abstraction of plastic and foam. He stared cross-eyed into the camera.

'You think that's intentional?'

'*Of course* it's intentional.'

Godzilla stopped to consider the 300,000-volt barrier, tilting his head in a distinctly human gesture of consideration. Guns and tanks shot at him; he roared irritatedly and was goaded into striking the barrier. Sparks flew off in various directions. Godzilla tangled with the wires, still roaring. Moments later, he had cleared the barrier and was newly equipped with fire-breathing properties. He stomped through the city-scape, exhaling fire (the fire was actually a thin, evanescent steam, due to understandable constraints within the special effects department) and setting the landscape alight with flames. Buildings were ablaze; bridges collapsed. A fire engine emitted a tinny whine as it wheeled ineffectually down a deserted side street.

The camera settled on a landscape of burning buildings, debris and rubble. The image was disturbingly realistic. In the centre stood Godzilla, in profile and in triumph. In a kind of appreciative slow-motion tribute, the camera showed Godzilla contemplating the city before turning his head and moving on. 'Godzilla has turned the heart of Tokyo into a sea of fire,' a journalist declared. 'Beneath the flames, thousands lie dead or dying.' Godzilla returned to the harbour, then disappeared into the ocean. Tokyo lay smouldering, a fire-ravaged ruin.

Looking closer at the screen, it became obvious that Tokyo looked, in fact, much as it looked following the American firebomb raids of the Second World War – one of the war's many mutual, many wanton, acts of killing that was not much remarked upon, nor much remembered. The mythic dimensions of Godzilla boiled down to the fact that he represented, with his foam and plastic costume and his steam-for-fire breath, the conflux of confused emotions following Japan's destruction and defeat in the war. Towering over that devastated landscape, he was a creature of contradiction and muddled allegory, confusedly trespassing upon matters as grave as those of nationalism, nuclear warfare, human brutality, guilt and shame.

In this way, what began as an overly simplistic allegory (in which Godzilla clearly represented the devastation of Japan in the final days of the Second

World War) grew a little confused as the film progressed. The identifications of the story became muddled, the narrative reasoning crumbled. Central to the trajectory of the story's emotional logic was the sympathy the audience was meant to feel for Godzilla, what my dad called 'the human aspect' to the monster. As the sympathetic elderly scientist declared, 'We shouldn't be killing him. We should be studying him.' Godzilla was unmistakably the story's (eponymous) hero, so much so that it was not too much to declare that Godzilla was not American or Allied after all, but intrinsically Japanese; that from his seeming indestructibility to his final, devastating end (which amounted to something of a cheap shot on the part of the government, entailing the desperate use of a scientific technology that had results disturbingly akin to those of the atomic bomb), Godzilla represented *Japan*'s experience during the war; and that in this character, much beleaguered and misunderstood and finally brought down, Japan saw some resemblance, however faint or distorted, to itself.

And it was maybe his quality of rage that made Godzilla so much an emblem of post-war Japan. The important thing about him was that the sympathy and identification we attached to him came about not despite, but rather because of, his anger. In the unlikely character of a radioactive monster, post-war Japanese society found an outlet for the anger that was not permissible elsewhere, the rage that could not be expressed in any more formal a conduit of culture than that of a monster movie. And thus a key contradiction was at the core of the relationship between Godzilla and the cultural imagination that bred him: Godzilla was at once the source of the unimaginable destruction that fell upon Japan during the war, and also the mouthpiece for the anger the Japanese felt during and after this destruction, an anger mostly half-silenced in its expression.

It was only a monster movie – and moreover one that, as much as it courted allegory, had not bothered to work out the totality of its inner logic. But that confusion, that narrative wreckage, was itself the symptom of a traumatized culture. And ultimately it was maybe in that fractured uncertainty, even more than in its topical inclinations, that the film became genuinely representative of Japan's post-war moral environment. Ambiguity was at the heart of post-war Japan. And as much as he maybe expressed the devastation of the bomb and Japan's latent outrage, Godzilla, in the double guise of perpetrator and victim, also represented the impossible guilt that scarred the Japanese psyche in the wake of the war – the guilt that was supreme cause and declaration of Japan's lasting wound.

Following their catastrophic defeat (two nuclear bombs, a Russian invasion, the Emperor's broadcast renunciation of the long-cherished myth of monarchical divinity, all crowded into a handful of days) and in the midst of an atmosphere thick with shame, many Japanese declared that their country was itself responsible for the dropping of the bomb, as a final consequence of its brutal aggression in the war. The accusation was first whispered, and then spoken and then ratified, and as the Japanese people grew obsessed with seeking out the measure of their own responsibility in the alien cataclysm that overcame their country, guilt overtook shame to become the chief indicator of the country's low morale.

In the figure of Godzilla, Japan's recent history was

articulated as travesty and tragedy but above all as a somehow self-inflicted catastrophe, the final outcome in a long course of self-destruction. It was perhaps in this last layering of significance that Godzilla attained his total, symbolic meaning. After all, he did not turn to foreign soil, but headed instead for native land. And if Godzilla was expressionless and lumbering, then that was because no amount of expression was going to capture the conflict of an intractable, shameful guilt that could not be reasoned with or hidden away. In the end, my dad was right – the lumbering, the awkwardness, all of that had to be seen as nothing less than intentional.

When he won the Nobel Prize for Literature in 1994, Kenzaburo Oe gave a speech entitled 'Japan, the Ambiguous, and Myself'. The title was his adaptation of Yasunari Kawabata's own 1968 Nobel acceptance speech, 'Japan, the Beautiful, and Myself', and it has an awkwardness entirely symptomatic of Oe's own probing relationship to language. As a writer, both in his themes and in his prose, Oe has perhaps always sacrificed the Beautiful in favour of the Ambiguous. And it is maybe the nature of this barter that has so much made him the foremost chronicler of the Japanese post-war experience. Across the varied body of his work, Kenzaburo Oe has written the consciousness of contemporary Japan, in all of its awkwardness and ambiguity.

The ambiguity chequered through Oe's prose, the jarring discontinuities and uncertainties of style, are resolutely laced and tied back to the historical consciousness of the nation, which is perhaps the transfiguring mechanism at work in his fiction. That sacrifice of the Beautiful for the Ambiguous is not simply a matter of stylistics, but is instead a forfeit deeply knit into the reality of contemporary Japan. In his award speech Oe declared, 'as someone living in present-day Japan . . . I cannot join Kawabata in saying "Japan, the Beautiful, and Myself" . . . it is only in terms of "Japan, the Ambiguous, and Myself" that I can talk about myself.' Oe specified the ambiguity that characterizes contemporary Japan as a tugging, historical polarization:

Japan is split between two opposite poles of ambiguity. This ambiguity, which is so powerful and penetrating that it divides both the state and its people, and affects me as a writer like a deep-felt scar, is evident in various ways. The modernization of Japan was oriented toward learning from and imitating the West, yet the country is situated in Asia and has firmly maintained its traditional culture . . . even in the West, to which its culture was supposedly quite open, it has long remained inscrutable or only partially understood.

In identifying that ambiguity as a polarization 'powerful and penetrating', as a 'deep-felt scar' and a force dividing 'both the state and its people', Oe identifies the chief trauma of Japan in the twentieth century, one that marks all the living generations: the onslaught of an unrelenting modernity that was imposed from without and unresolved within. Oe traces the effect of that trauma from its original imposition in the 'opening up' of the country to the West, through to Japan's brutal aggression in the war and onward to the dropping of the two atomic bombs. It is the context and the framing for the atomic aftermath.

That trauma is also the chief cause behind the failure

of Japan's collective memory, and the dark spots of amnesia that crowd through it. It is in relation to that essentially traumatized, densely fractured memory that Oe best understands what it means to be Japanese; he describes himself as 'a citizen of a nation that in the recent past was stampeded into "insanity in enthusiasm for destruction" both on its own soil and on that of neighboring nations'; he describes the status of being Japanese as 'sharing bitter memories of the past'. Those memories are unsorted, essentially unreadable. They are beyond paper history or stone monument. The bomb – the gross manifestation of a foreign culture – and the war that preceded it perhaps represent the apex of the trauma Oe speaks of. But they also extended the lifespan of that trauma by reducing the country's memories into barely legible fragments; it is the legacy of those broken memories that today continues to dictate the providence of the nation, producing the shape of apologies still unsaid, and recompenses not yet fully made.

Oe has often written in praise of those who 'acknowledge clearly that Japan and the Japanese were aggressors in the Pacific War that brought on the atomic bombings'. If narrative – the ability to piece together and make sense of illegible fragments, the ability to tell stories of oneself, to oneself – promises a recovery from trauma, then Oe's chosen narrative of healing is, inevitably and unchangeably, that of guilt. Guilt is the story he follows, confession the healing he envisages. It is, after all, towards the task of facing up to and even elongating this feeling of guilt that much of Oe's writing is directed. The body of his literature, and in particular his fictional works (those great novels of abandonment and neglect, doubt and uncertainty, *A Quiet Life* or *A Personal Matter*), is deeply marked by the furrows of guilt, and it is in that marking that its historical context is shown. The lasting enigma of Hiroshima was the guilt it brought showering down upon all involved, the guilt from which even its victims could not be exempt.

After the outrage, the rancour and the bitterness and the sheer impossibility of the events that ended the war, it was the ambiguity and the guilt that remained. Guilt was the lasting residue of the infamous black rain that fell across Japan in the final days of the Second World War, and the story of Japan's guilt was the story told to and by a country that was broken beyond repair, and had little hope of healing. But the narrative of guilt that replicated itself across Japan, in hushed conversations and low-hung heads, in letters and in essays, in monuments and in the changing of a moral guard, was perhaps itself a result of the bipolar split Oe speaks of – itself a consequence of Japan's torn and uncertain moral alliances, its tugging polarization between East and West. And if that guilt was a symptom of Japan's chronic ambiguity, the enduring question that would have to be considered was whether symptom can ever also function as cure.

Sure enough, as the event of the bombings receded into the past, the disjunction between the proposed recovery and its actual reality grew more pronounced, and the matter of healing became more complicated. At first and in the interim, when healing seemed a thing of hopefulness and peace a matter of willingness, guilt seemed the only thing of certainty. In 1952, at the heart of the Hiroshima Peace Memorial Park (the naming was significant – those two words at the centre, 'peace' and 'memorial', couched in so close together and speaking of a passing of peace that became permanent on 6 August 1945), a stone coffin containing a list of the 100,000 then known victims of the A-bomb was placed under the sheltering arc of a memorial cenotaph. On the coffin, the following words were inscribed:

> Let all the souls here rest in peace;
> For we shall not repeat the evil.

The inscription was a memorial of mourning, but more than that it was a penance and a definite proclamation of guilt, for only a country wholly persuaded in the matter of its own culpability would couch the count of its dead in the swathing of a self-professed guilt. Perhaps that apparent conviction was brokered by the hope that in proclaiming their guilt and their loud resolution never to 'repeat the evil', they could somehow prevent catastrophe from blackening their skies again; perhaps it was not the fact or truth of guilt, but rather the gesture of confession and repentance that was the more important. For all these many reasons and in all these many ways, there seemed to be a safety and healing in the repeated declaration of a guilt literally set in stone. And it was in this way that guilt overcame outrage, as sorrow's only midwife.

Eventually, though, guilt became a burst dam, a faulty solution and situation, and once sorrow was fully birthed and outrage returned, that guilt had to be reconsidered. It was in the notorious 'Inscription Dispute' that the Japanese would formally begin to question the validity of that guilt. Key questions emerged: who was the 'we' implied in the inscription? Who was it that needed to claim responsibility for 'the evil' that was never to be repeated? The questions were nightmarish in the certainty they demanded, the ambiguity they would not allow. The problems of guilt, which had for so long lain concealed beneath Japan's ambiguity, beneath the country's confused and mottled identity, finally emerged in the fullness of their genuine complexity.

Two opposing camps formed: the Inscription Correction Society, and the Inscription Defending Society. The Inscription Correction Society held that the cenotaph inscription, with the guilt it declared and the deference towards the West it implied, was 'blasphemous' to the memory of those listed on the register of the dead; the Inscription Defending Society insisted that the inscription simply protested against the revival of militaristic nationalism, and the renewed onslaught of war. It was the polarization between innocence and guilt, chaos and certainty, and the issue at the heart of that dispute was the nature of the bomb's totality itself. It was a question of whether the bomb, with its capacity for complete eradication, absolved the Japanese of the history of their former war crimes, or showered the country in a guilt so complete it could not be avoided or undone. The dispute was never wholly resolved, and instead represented a permanent blind spot in the memory of the nation, a growing chasm that was like a discreet revolution turned upon Oe's 'two opposite poles of ambiguity'.

Ten years after the dropping of the bomb, America was in turn seeking out its own narrative of guilt and expiation, and then suddenly these matters were no longer solely Japan's to debate. There is always this alternate history to be evoked: the possibility that in that first painful admission of guilt, a real loss of American innocence might have occurred, and the country experienced something like a tardy coming of age. But as it was, guilt's darkness was quickly cleared (waiting, perhaps, for other events that were still to come, trials that were still in the making), and the fundamental buoyancy of American innocence re-asserted. America's quest for guilt was, then, particularly American, and it reached its epitome when mid-century America stumbled and then seized upon a most unlikely hero. It was through this dubious idol that the American conscience would learn the recompenses of guilt, and also those of expiation.

In the course of those turbulent mid-century years, Texan pilot Claude Eatherly grew famous for a clear morning sky – the sky over Japan on 6 August 1945. There are never very many clouds over Japan in August, but the clear sky over Hiroshima on that day was a clear sky full of fateful, monumental importance. At sunrise on that day, Eatherly's plane *Straight Flush* reached the edges of open air over Hiroshima. It was closely followed by the *Enola Gay*, the plane carrying the atom bomb. The *Straight Flush* made a simulated bomb run over Hiroshima, taking note of visibility, before radioing back to headquarters the following message: 'Cloud cover less than 3/10ths at all altitudes.

Advice: Bomb Primary.' Approximately fifty minutes later, the bomb was dropped on Hiroshima.

It was maybe the deadliest weather report in history. But what immortalized Claude Eatherly as the Hiroshima Pilot was not the fatal accuracy of his report or its terrifyingly reticent advice, but rather the way Eatherly himself became at once a symbol for mass guilt, a cathartic cipher of jumbled signals and signs, a fraud, a hero, an icon and a petty criminal. In a decade of tumultuous announcements and events – the suicide of Hitler, the birth of the United Nations, the rise of McCarthyism – Eatherly's much contested declaration that he had been drawn to a life of petty crime because he was seeking 'punishment' for his involvement in Hiroshima seemed as incredible, and as significant, as the rest.

After being dismissed by the Air Force and seeing his marriage fail, Eatherly took to a life of swash-buckling petty crime: a binge of forgery and fraud in New Orleans, theatrical hold-ups in Texas that were almost comical in their lack of palpable intent, brief bouts in prison. In all this Eatherly seemed just another battle-torn war vet, unable to adjust to civilian life and civilian expectation. He was checked in and out of mental institutions, and diagnosed with, variously, battle fatigue, schizophrenia, and finally, more than ten years after Hiroshima, a classic guilt complex.

It was in this last diagnosis that the symbolic character of Claude Eatherly finally became legible to the world. The real mystery of Claude Eatherly – the illegibility of the pilot nicknamed 'Poker Face', the question of his meaningless crimes, his mental instability, his recklessness and the catastrophic failure of his dreams – was dispelled once and for all when the lexicon of guilt was laid over the disparate tangles of his life. Over radio telegrams and newspapers that ran several times round the globe, the world grew to understand that Eatherly's spiral into mental instability and a capricious life of crime was in fact a longing to draw justice from a system that refused to penalize him for what he perceived to be his great, capital crime: his involvement in the bombing of Hiroshima.

The legends grew apace with the myth – that Claude Eatherly had attempted suicide upon hearing President Truman's order to continue development of the hydrogen bomb, that he refused to touch his pension from the Air Force, declaring that it was 'blood money', that he sent money every month to the victims of Hiroshima, with hand-written notes reading 'Forgive me'. That Claude Eatherly was a political prisoner, the American Dreyfus, confined to a lunatic asylum by a malevolent government conspiracy. The real Claude Eatherly disappeared into the ultimate *cause célèbre* that even Bertrand Russell couldn't resist endorsing. The truths and the facts of Claude Eatherly became irrelevant as he ceased his ordinary human existence as a man built up of history and fact, and began his almost divine existence as a creation of public need.

Claude Eatherly was never much more than a chimera, summoned forth to address the national need for a symbol of guilt and the collective longing for expiation. He was the marker of a movement, tracking as he did the way guilt finally spread its way West, and the historical moment when the world as a whole was at last prepared to confront the matter of its guilt. But he also recorded the poverty of insight that was brought to that confrontation, and reflected the way its complexities were imagined and then reduced to the simpler terms of catharsis. It was the obliterating extremity of Eatherly's feeling that was to endure as his most meaningful characteristic. He may have fraudulently represented the truth behind his life of petty crime. But in the end, the only important truth was that the public at large caught hold of Eatherly because they too were seeking the forgetfulness of total atonement.

In the heyday of his celebrity, his advocates insisted that Eatherly was a 'Hiroshima victim too'. In retrospect, that identification outrages all sense of proportion and propriety. The case of Claude Eatherly, with its many revelations and stunning reversals, became a spectacular example of a misguided hysteria of emotion. It became an example of the convenience that can be cloaked in guilt, the disappointment and selfishness that can be concealed in penance; it reminded us that one half of catharsis is in the forgetting. In Claude Eatherly, the code of catharsis and the mantra of guilt were finally jammed, and then fell away into illegibility.

It was thus, in the passageways of guilt, that we,

both in America and Japan, forgot how to remember Hiroshima, and lost sight of the atomic aftermath that continues, even today.

We disembark from the train and enter into the last days of what will be remembered as the year of the tsunami, the year of the long, sleepless war, the year of women murdered in their last term and children kidnapped while sleeping, the year of the most important election of our lifetime and the worst election of our lifetime. Rarely has a year been so ready to end, and when it does finally reach its end, we find that we too are exhausted, for these brief days with my grandmother have been more taxing than we can allow ourselves to admit. On the last day of that exhausted year a heavy snow falls across Western Japan. It starts in the afternoon; from our hotel window I watch first a light sprinkling that could be mistaken for rain, then repeated flurries of heavy flakes that accumulate on the pavement, on the roads and on the low sloping eaves of the houses.

In the morning of the New Year, the snow is there still, and everything is quiet. On a triangular patch of snow-coated land, apex bordered by a low and reluc-tant river, the Hiroshima Peace Memorial Park is deserted, nothing more than unbroken yards of an approximate white, falling into the peaks and troughs of quiet monuments. At the southern end of the park the Hiroshima Peace Memorial Museum and Conference Centre is closed; the shops and restaurants near by are shut up. The trains run irregularly if at all, the streetcars rattle by empty, and there is, it seems, no reason to be here.

In the cold, the statues and cenotaphs wear their abandonment lightly. Shapes and figures shrouded in a slow-melting whiteness, they have the modesty of ancient ruins. From the northern tip of the park and across the river, the real, the literal, remnants of Hiroshima's ruins are visible: the tall skeleton of a dome, snow slipping down its ribs, piles of crumbled brick and stone half concealed. A tacked-up sign: 'No Entry'.

I look at it from a distance, from across this river that bore the bloated bodies of the dead; never have ruins seemed still so close to the moment of their destruction. Broken abutments, fallen staircases and

blown-out walls, the immaculately preserved frag-
ments of an inarticulate past, frozen into a permanence
that is quietly, trenchantly, deceitful. Past that quiet-
ness emerges the truth: that this seeming historicity is
maybe the most deceptive thing about the memorials
scattered through the park; the most deceptive thing
about the museum, with the uncontained count of its
atomic rubble (a wristwatch shattered and stopped at
8:15, a bit of twisted wire and a popped out lens, a
scorched shirt scarred by black rain); about the ceno-
taph, with its hidden list of growing names. However
much buried in stone and monument and inscription,
the day's past power finds a rupture into the present.
The past cannot contain it; it breaks out, it escapes,
until it is all around the park, almost sixty years later
and on a cold New Year's Day.

There is nothing safe about this place. There is
nothing peaceful about this place that, sixty years
ago, sat at the epicentre of history's most destructive
man-made explosion.

Breathing in coldness, I continue to look out at the
ruined building with its burnt-out dome. The Hiro-
shima Industrial Promotion Hall, now known as the

A-bomb Dome, is in a sense the chief material witness to the destructiveness of the atomic bomb. An incontrovertible record of the absolute physical levelling that was meted out upon the city, it is a building that bears witness, in its torn and wrecked limbs, in the measure of its half-life. Built in 1915, it was, in its original incarnation, a symbol of Western modernism. Designed by a renowned Czech architect, the hall was, with its proud dome of coppery-green, its solid walls and its multiple staircases, an emblem of modern industry. Then the bomb dropped, leaving behind a pale wreckage banked against empty spaces, and the Industrial Promotion Hall began its second life as the A-bomb Dome.

The A-bomb Dome, like all ruins, is on the one hand a statement partially made and half-destroyed, on the other a statement that attains its total meaning only through its fractured, incomplete state, as a symbol of the fallout from Japan's historical polarization. However emblematic of the Second World War and the dropping of the atomic bomb, the A-bomb Dome also represents, with its historical association of industry and progress, Japan's experience since the onslaught of a too abrupt modernity that one day slammed into the landscape of the country, carving its space out in hard and bumpy ridges. It is by the lines of this historical continuity that these ruins represent the stalled building projects of the Japanese Nineties, the physical detritus of the Bubble era, the muted apathy of a youth generation that bears its scars on the inside. They will continue to bear this significance until the time when that ambiguity and that polarization are somehow resolved, or laid to uneasy rest.

I turn away from the Dome, and walk southwards towards the centre of the park. In the acute silence, in the grey light that renders everything washed and worn, the park has the look of a place already fading out from the front rows of history and the relevance of memory. Along the riverbank a woman spins across the paved road, bicycle wheels whirring gently. With a sputtering of wings, a pair of fat black crows sail across the park and settle on the embankment, heads bobbing.

A few minutes later I pass an elderly man. His head is down, but there is an energetic purposefulness to his gait, a muted air of physical health that suddenly converts the park into an ordinary place. In the rhythm of his stride the Memorial Park becomes simply one aspect, one portion, of the Hiroshima that did not flare into being in the early morning hours of 6 August 1945, but that existed for centuries preceding that infamous date, and that has continued its existence in the face of impossible horror for the many decades that followed. A city cannot always be remembering, the man's posture seems to say as he moves by, edging carefully past pockets of slick snow; a city has a right, not to forget or to move on, but at least to continue.

The man and I take opposing routes, parting ways without having kept company, and I arrive at the Memorial Cenotaph by way of one of the park's central paths. The coffin, and its inscription, is tucked sheltering beneath the low arc of the monument; protected, hidden away, its dimensions easily measured. And it occurs to me that what is crucial here is not what is revealed, but what is concealed. A formal register of the dead, a listing of names so extensive that it could not be witnessed, but instead had to be closed away, the ritual of listing itself a symptom as old and battered as the trauma it bore testament to. If it is impossible to find the story of Hiroshima, then that is because it is in so many ways a place beyond story or narrative.

And that is the paradox of the Memorial Park, and of all those who visit or seek it. It cannot serve its function, without desecrating its purpose. We come here to remember, and find that we can remember nothing; we find that even the conjectures and hypotheses of imagining are impossible. Memory, guilt, healing and recovery – the clichés of the imagination do not function here; they lack ballast in a place that is drained of all those elements that give narrative its density and function. In the end, it is not the clichés that persist, but the unexpected blankness of a place so thickly written, so thronged with association. It is the shock of a blankness that is, after so many years, still so unmitigated.

There is, it seems, nothing to be said. Blankness and incomprehension are as simple as a monument covered in snow, a raw patch of dirt and dead grass, a continued coldness in the air. I have no real idea what I am doing here.

A little later, riding the train back to Osaka, sitting with my head against the velour seat, mind wandering and eyes looking out across a landscape slowly colouring from white to green, I stumble upon two memories of the time I spent in Japan as a child, forgotten fragments now unexpectedly returned. They are matched, in the timing of their arrival, against the vast monument of the past so recently stood before me, but clothed in a contrasting intimacy and warmth. And though there is thus no real proximity of thought or validity of association, that disparate pairing is somehow made, gaining in substance, growing concrete, and then, through those mysterious and unknown means, finally setting fast.

The shutter flashes open. I am with my mother at my grandparents' house, which is also confusingly my uncle's house and the house where my cousins live, so that there is always a great frenzy of people present – my three cousins, my uncle who looks like my mother, except that all the features of his face are slightly more slack, his jowls loosening into soft folds of skin and his eyes disappearing into the wrinkles of his smile. His wife, always smiling, stares serenely as her children run shrieking around her, jumping over tables and brandishing expensive toys carelessly.

My mother is seated with her sister (she has a lively face that is the opposite of my uncle's, all the features resolving into an overall impression of tidiness, from the bright round eyes and the small pursed mouth to the economical movements of her head, so that together my mother and her siblings represent three separate gradients of the same face) at a low table in the middle of the room. I remember this room exactly. The altar for the ancestors in one corner of the room, with its candles and its crumbling incense ashes and its tiny carved stands for offerings of sweets and fruits. The small brass vase for flowers, the photographs of my great-grandparents and their great-grandparents, propped up and peering at us out of strangely familiar faces. The impassive row of cabinets, a sheath of gleaming black lacquer casting shadows that no amount of electric light can dispel. But I cannot remember anything else about the house, not the stairs that must have taken us to that room, which I know distinctly to be on the second floor, not the rooms upstairs, nor the street outside – nothing.

My mother reaches a hand forward for her cup of tea, moving her arm carefully around my head, which is resting along her hip, my fingers grasping childish handfuls of skirt. My auntie tilts her head and murmurs something to me, her voice rising up into a gentle interrogation point. My mother strokes my hair and says something in reply. My eyes are closed in drowsiness, and I am almost entirely asleep when my cousins troop in and look at me with eyes that are not hostile, nor uninterested, but simply unfriendly. They look at me and I look at them through heavy lids and for a long moment we regard each other. Then they retreat to the banks of leather sofas, shouting meaninglessly as they bounce from cushion to cushion, claw at an armrest, jump up and down, until at last my aunt turns to them and reprimands them sharply.

The door swings open and in comes my grandfather. He is tall, and on the frame of his broad shoulders and narrow waist he wears a deftly tailored suit. He is very handsome (family pictures examined later in life corroborate this first memory, which is like a first impression despite the fact that he has a time-worn familiarity as he comes into the room). But it is not simply the strong and regular features of his face, the bright eyes and the thick hair and the determined chin; it is not just the easy movements of his body as he strides forward. Rather there is a vitality to him that expresses itself as a good-natured charisma, an over-riding optimism that no amount of material success can match or artificially produce.

It is an isolated memory, and so I am not entirely sure how it is that I know he is my grandfather, but I do. And I am awed and enchanted by his magic. He stands there, fiddling with one hand through the change in his pockets and doing nothing at all beyond looking, and yet it seems impossible to recognize that he is a blood relation, that we are related not simply by the hazards of situation but by the stronger, more durable links of kin.

Both my mother and aunt bridle in his presence, yet smile despite themselves, and my cousins subdue their raucousness. But he is preoccupied with something, busy on his way elsewhere. As his eyes travel over the disparate array of his brood, they pass fleetingly over me. He blinks his eyes once, as if in surprise. Then it is only one moment more before he is gone again, taking with him that tremendous sense of organized vitality.

The shutter opens again. A train carriage slices through an unidentified landscape. The clock is set too fast and the tempo of everything, from the birds that fly from post to post to the whirring of the bicycles as they tumble down the roads, moves a touch too quickly. Laundry is hung out to dry over balcony railings, limp with assumed despair. Faces flash up: an old lady laughing with the postman, a young girl jiggling an ankle nervously as a boy leans closer. Then, gradually, the frame slows until it resolves into the picture of some anonymous bit of city, unremarked beyond its placid tenacity.

I cannot locate the place. Where is it – in Tokyo? Where my mother's parents live? Or in Osaka, maybe, where my father is from? Either way, the landscape is utterly anonymous, but also decidedly Japanese in a way that has nothing to do with the foreign characters that dot the signs, nothing to do with the raven hair and the pale skin that uniformly unites the collected figures in the street. In that instant of dislocation, my mind springs forwards twenty years and then backwards two weeks, to the train at the start of my journey, the train running from Narita Airport to Tokyo. And as I remember that past act of gazing out the window and wondering at the way everything – not just the signs and the architecture, but the trees, the quality of the light, the formation of the clouds – all pointed to the nature of place in the same way, the two moments cross over into one, like delicate transparencies laid one upon the other, two separate images overlapping to create a single image, the purposeful image.

The carriage is drenched in the kind of light that is so harsh as to be pure white, and I remember squinting in its brilliance. It splashes across the walls of the carriage, down onto the floor. All the colours in the train seem to fade out into the whiteness of that brighter summer's day. For a moment the passengers' clothing dulls into a discoloured palette, and the forest-green of the train seats fades into a candy-mint colour. Beside me, by some strange trick of light, my mother's hair appears almost white, and she closes her eyes to the light.

Nothing else. A final flash of light, and then the

shutter closes. And that is all. As the train rattles away from Hiroshima and on towards Osaka, a mechanical voice announces the next destination. I settle further into my seat. A young woman in a grey ruffled apron pushes a cart through the aisles, hawking wares of ice cream and canned coffee. As she exits the carriage a flurry of air sweeps through the doors, touched with the smell of snow outside, the train's slow and un-expected creaking; the dense trampling of feet on pavement, of passengers climbing on board, faces muffled in jackets and scarves.